I AM
NUMBER 8

For Aventer Gray

Contents

Foreword

By Joel Osteen

The Scriptures give many examples of people who did not think much of themselves, yet God called them to do something great. Moses, Gideon, and David were just such people. When God told Moses, perhaps the greatest prophet of the Old Testament, to bring the Israelites out of captivity, Moses said, "God, I'm ordinary. Pharaoh will never listen to me. I stutter." Gideon, when instructed by God's angel to stop farming and lead an army against the enemy, responded by saying, "How can I do that? I come from the poorest family. I am the least of my father's house." When the prophet Samuel came to anoint one of Jesse's sons to be the next king of Israel, Jesse thought so little of his youngest son, David, that he didn't even bother to bring him in from the fields where he was taking care of the sheep.

I believe that we might not have heard the names of Moses, Gideon, or David had they continued to see themselves the way others saw them. Instead, each of them changed their mind-set and began to see themselves as God saw them—as a liberator, a general, and a king.

Psychologists have long known that we will most often behave in a manner that is in harmony with the way we perceive ourselves. Proverbs 23:7 tells us that we become what we think about. This book is an important step in understanding this and more. My good friend John Gray reaches deep within himself to offer you an honest and humorous look at what it means to overcome those hardships, obstacles, and temptations that stand in the way of your true calling.

When you look at John Gray, you see a mighty man of God whose influence and ministry are among the fastest growing in the world today. You see a man who is sought after around the globe for his wisdom, his dynamic speaking style, and his great insights into God's Word. When you see what John has become, it is hard to imagine that there were ever any giants that stood in his way. Yet, as an only child in a fatherless home, he was dismissed by many as just an insignificant, buck-toothed kid. He was easily forgotten when his classmates were sending invitations and overlooked when choosing teams. But it was from that place of difficulty that John answered God's call to be a voice for those who feel lost, forgotten, and lonely. It was from that isolation that he now engages with millions in a ministry that continues to thrive and change the world around us.

I encourage you to read every word, consider every thought, and enjoy every laugh along the way as he takes you on a personal journey that will not only encourage you, but also will challenge you to rise up and claim the destiny that God has planned for you.

Introduction

It happened on a Friday night in Smithfield, Rhode Island.

When I think of revival, I rarely think of any city located in the northeast corridor of the United States. Don't close the book, northeasterners, let me explain! I can admit that in my shortsightedness at the time, I really could only imagine something like this happening in one of the southern states—mostly, the Bible Belt. Places where there is a history of these kinds of moments happening. In truth, nobody was looking for the Spirit of God to unify an entire generation in the middle of Rhode Island. Who really goes to Rhode Island to find destiny? And yet, I was so very wrong. Destiny is exactly what happened in Rhode Island. For the kids who attended that youth conference, and for me.

It was so chilly that day I could see my breath when I got out of the car. As I walked the short distance to the church, I could hear the sound of kids singing praise songs over a heavy bass-driven beat. I couldn't make out the exact song but I discerned the sound of passion. Kids don't fake passion these days. I know hunger when I hear it. These kids? These kids wanted more.

I was raised in church. My mom was a church pianist. Granny was too. My dad was a jazz organist. *That's* another story I'll get to later. My point is, I've been in church all my life. I'm also an observer. Those two things mean that I can clearly tell the difference between surface religious performance and authentic passion. The sound I heard on that cold day was the real thing. But even the sound could not have prepared me for the moment I would find myself in an hour later.

After the worship, I walked onto the platform. The kids were so excited, so passionate, the roar of the crowd was deafening. There were at least fifteen hundred youths and adults present, all staring up at me in anticipation of what God might do next. The atmosphere was amazing. As I began the message, I could hear the sound again, only this time, it was a rumbling. My words started flowing in a way they had never before. I was in a *moment*. As a communicator, as a preacher, you can tell when you're in a *moment*. There have been many times when I have preached and could feel that I was hitting up against something in the atmosphere—whether it was the audience's curiosity or their resistance to what I was sharing, based on whatever differences they brought with them (denominational perspectives and theology, etc.).

But these kids connected to me, and I connected to

them. There was something more I needed to say. I started reading from 1 Samuel 16. I shared with them that the Old Testament prophet Samuel had gone into the city of Bethlehem and to the house of Jesse to anoint the future King of Israel. After seeing seven of Jesse's sons, Samuel asked the man, "Are all the young men here?" Jesse said, "Well, there is the youngest" (1 Sam. 16:11). There was someone, another son, that Jesse had forgotten.

From that moment in the sermon, there was a shift. I started sharing about a young man—David—relegated to the fields, hidden in his own home, reviled by his brothers, overlooked by his father, but still very much loved and seen by God. Samuel goes on to say in the passage, "Send for him; we won't sit down until he comes" (1 Sam. 16:11). Jesse calls David, who was doing what he was always doing, watching the sheep. He didn't realize that everything was about to change.

I shared this story with kids from hardscrabble neighborhoods and not-so-great circumstances. I shared it because I was convinced that God wanted to tell them that even though people may not see or acknowledge their gifts, that did not mean He didn't place those gifts in them. They were hidden for a reason and a season, but they were there, deep down inside, just beneath the surface.

I don't know if I was really prepared for how much this message would resonate. Kids leaned forward in their seats. Folks who were texting at the beginning, stopped. Before I knew it, I had everybody's attention. God was moving.

With each beat, with each point, I could feel this passion welling up. I could feel this intensity, this hunger where I was connecting with a group of kids who, for any number of reasons, identified as the forgotten, the overlooked, and the undervalued.

I continued to talk about David, his life, how it seemed that he came out of nowhere, that nobody saw him. I later learned that this was true for many of the kids in that audience. They believed nobody saw them. Some of them came from broken homes; others had their dreams shattered, or innocence snatched. Yet in that moment, they found a collective hope. They realized that none of the negative things, none of the forgotten things, could stop God from choosing them.

I pushed the sermon further. I talked about how God prepares the forgotten; how He equips the undervalued and sets them in high places for His purpose. This was true for all of them—the broken, the fatherless, the motherless, the ones who had never once heard they had inherent value. Tears flowed. Kids flocked to the altar all on their own. A sound entered the room I had never heard before, and that's when I knew that this was not just a sermon, it was a movement.

The idea that David, the 8th son of no one, was not just a historical figure from thousands of years ago who just so happened to be biblical legend, but his story, the story of a number 8, the number of new beginnings in biblical numerology, could resonate so deeply with thirteen-year-old kids from Rhode Island was amazing. The fact that this same story resonated with me, the then forty-one-year-old man preaching about it, was a revelation.

The sermon wasn't just for them. It was also for me. I needed to be reminded that the place where I stood in that moment was not because I deserved it or had worked to attain it. Rather I had been given that platform by a God who had spotted me deep in the recesses of a little, working-class neighborhood in Cincinnati, Ohio, and declared that I had value. God declared that I had purpose, even though I did not have a father there to teach me that. My heavenly Father declared it and my mother made sure I knew it.

I wasn't just a kid that everybody laughed at because I had buck teeth and alopecia. I wasn't just a kid who couldn't get a date. I wasn't just the goofy virgin with acne. I was more than that. God hid me for a reason. God didn't keep me from things; he kept me *for* a thing. I wasn't just preaching to these kids about the number 8; I *was* a number 8. And so were many of them.

Maybe, just maybe, so are you.

You're looking for something.

What you've done before is not working.

What you're doing now is good, but you know you can live at a higher level. You're a youth and want to know that serving God will really help you in those tough alone places.

You're a talented young adult who believes you have a future, but you just can't see it—things just aren't working out the way you expected.

You have a family, but can't seem to see God in the details of every day. It's rough trying to keep it all together, right?

Maybe you are eighteen. Maybe you are eighty. Whatever your age, your life has purpose today. And yes, I realize that your real questions may have nothing to do with age. You want to know how to keep from feeling discouraged when you don't fit? You toy with the idea that no one would care if you just gave up. You wonder if you really do matter.

I want you to know that you are not alone. I know how you feel. We are number 8s. We are the ones with shaky knees and sweaty palms even when we are at the top of our game because we feel like an imposter. We are the ones who may not even be in the game; we're sitting on the sidelines, waiting to be invited in.

But here's another truth: We are also the ones who will not give up, who will not be overlooked, who will not let shame, guilt, and fear hold us back. David, the number 8 son, a lowly shepherd, was anointed by God and became king. I, being a man who has felt the pain of being an outsider, also used my pain for the purpose of serving God.

That chilly Friday in Rhode Island, I shared the story of David, a man after God's own heart, the eighth son, and how he was able to move from shepherd boy to king of a nation despite being rejected and marginalized. Much of the time, David was afraid—just like many of us. But fear doesn't change God's plan for us. David was a number 8. I am a number 8. And you just might be a number 8 too. If you are, then I can assure you that your release is near. Your story is in these pages. This book is for you.

Throughout this book, I will share with you my own personal journey. Being on a pastoral team that serves an average of forty-five thousand people each Sunday, speaking at global events, and being blessed with a loving wife and two children, I have come a long way from my experiences as a child. The initial chapters will examine David's life from his days in the field as a shepherd to his time as king when, like I have on many days, David said to God, "I can't believe I'm here. What did I do to deserve this honor?" David had not always been honest. He had cheated and lied and even murdered. But God kept his promise that David would be great. Being a number 8 means that you are not expected to be perfect, but simply to love God and live in your purpose.

I also want to highlight the value of preparation and training for number 8s. It's critical that we are ready when God does decide to remove us from isolation. God opened the door for David to be chosen by Saul as his armor bearer. David was not from a royal family nor was he famous, but he was chosen. God had already chosen him, and now King Saul had also selected David to play for him to relieve distress.

Another important point for number 8s to remember

is that what looks like "suddenly" is the result of patience over time. Ever hear of the phrase "a twenty-year overnight success"? Exactly. I will explore in future chapters what it means to be patient and wait for God to open a door or opportunity. Whether you are retired by the time you "suddenly" achieve success or young, when time may seem to be moving way too slowly for your taste, patience is going to be necessary when it appears that your dreams have been deferred, delayed, blocked, and derailed.

It gets exhausting being a number 8—being turned down over and over, though you know you are ready for the fight. But when it's time to step up, it's critical that we do exactly that. Yes, there may be people who have been around longer, have more money, fame, or connections. David's brothers did not want David to fight the Philistine Goliath.

Maybe it was because they loved him, but maybe it was because they thought he might win and make them look bad. Regardless of why David's brothers wanted to stop him, David did not allow them to keep him from taking care of his business. He kept asking until the word got to Saul and he was granted permission to fight on behalf of their cause.

Just like David's faith in God's ability to bring victory against Goliath, through his meager weapons, I have always relied on God, even as a child. Many of the events that might have made me take an easier path were only overcome by the grace and strength of God. There were periods when people disappointed me and I had to fight my own "giants." However, you can overcome giants when you believe that you are not going into battle alone.

Recognize that we all have giants. We all face severe hardships, seemingly insurmountable obstacles and temptations. We all have problems. We all have temptations. While it is true we all have giants, it is also true that every giant can be defeated. After all, giants rarely start out that way.

Goliath was not always a giant. He was not always nine feet six inches tall. He was once a baby. And with the passing of time and the nurture he received from others, the baby became a child. And the child became a teenager. And the teenager became a man. And the man turned into a giant.

In the same way, giants often begin quite small. When we have a big sin in our lives, it started as a little sin that was allowed, nurtured, fed, and even encouraged, and then became a giant that taunts us. It started with a so-called Christian liberty that we proclaimed and is now getting the best of us. In time, little things become big things.

Another point I will explore: Prayer and praise—worshipping God—overcomes fear. Time and time again in Scripture, we see that Saul, the first king of Israel, appears to be afraid of David. Yes, this tall warrior was afraid of the young man David. The truth is, when you worship God and are in communion with God, you can make even strong kings and leaders afraid. Mostly, they are afraid because you are not. They see your unwavering trust in

God and it makes them nervous. Isaiah 54:17 says that "no weapon formed against you shall prosper." Worship keeps you sane as you trust that this word from the Lord is true.

Your blind spots, those places of sin that you can't see or don't know about, can often lead you into the wilderness called failure. Ah, *failure.* The word no one wants to hear connected with their name. I hope to remind you in these pages of the value of failure. It's in this particular wilderness that number 8s pick up clues on how to lead, love, and serve in the worst of times. David finds himself in the wilderness a few times in Scripture. At one point, he is not even alone. He has four hundred men who have followed him into the wilderness. That can happen. In the wilderness, we need others to encourage, support, admonish, and defend us. David had a community in his life to point out his blind spots in love. Despite it being one of the worst times in David's life, God knew the wilderness was an opportunity for David to get himself together. To learn some new stuff. I have found myself in the failure wilderness, and so have you. Numbers 8s learn valuable lessons from failure because they know that even kings and queens fail. This is particularly true when it comes to relationships.

Whether it was his first wife, Michal, his failure with Bathsheba, or his lazy fathering, David was not able to navigate the land mines of personal relationships well. That's a common trait of number 8s though. I have to make a conscious decision daily to give attention to my personal relationships in the same way I give attention to the call on my life: the travels, the meetings, the preaching, the serving others. It certainly isn't easy.

There are challenges and victories in making a commitment to relationships and staying faithful to them. Which leads me to another critical point for you to remember as you read: Numbers 8s aren't always successful at getting it right. But they keep trying.

In the final chapters of the book, I wrestle with the pain of growing up without a father or father figure. David also missed something in his relationship with his father. Everything in David's life, good and bad, can be traced back to that relationship. In ancient Israel, it was the duty of the father to declare identity, and yet, David was anointed king of Israel in front of a father who seems to have never seen him.

My hope is that this book will offer some practical application to your everyday life. I hope that the illustrations and personal testimonies will run parallel to areas in your own life and challenge you to identify where you are when it comes to your calling. Too many times people think of a "calling" as something that happens only in the context of a preaching ministry. But I believe that nurses have a calling. Botanists have a calling. Bus drivers have a calling. I still remember my bus driver from ninth grade. He wore glasses and was bald on the top with hair on the sides. He was a kind man and always had a good word for me when I got on the bus. I looked forward to seeing him because he encouraged me. If he saw me running for the bus, he'd stop. He saw something in me very early on. This man was walking in his calling for that season of his life with a kind of excellence that pleased God. Without a doubt, being called to something is a supernatural thing, only not in the spooky way we often think of it. It simply means doing what we can in the natural, and trusting God for the "super."

So there's not too much difference between David and me. Or you and David. Or you and me. David was a shepherd in the field. I delivered pizza. You may have (fill in the blank). But when we realize we have the favor of God on our lives, we can go from being a shepherd boy to a deliverer of a nation; a delivery boy to shepherding thousands every week. From wherever you are today, to wherever God wants to take you tomorrow. From one number 8 to another, I want this book to challenge you to claim that destiny. David was born in Bethlehem. His family wasn't special. No one saw him coming. Yet by the time it was all said and done, the nation and the world would never be the same! A king had taken the throne! And so it goes with you. This is the ultimate power of a number 8. The glory that is produced in us is hidden until the exact moment it's needed.

When I set out to share this word, I often wondered how many others have felt overlooked and forgotten. I don't have the exact statistics, but here's what I know for sure: If you are someone who has felt like your life carries no intrinsic, inherent value, this book is for you. In truth, this book is for all of us. This book is for me. Again, I am number 8 and so are you. God's about to reveal to you a purpose so necessary, so critical, so essential that he had to hide it behind pain, grief, and misunderstanding in order to protect it until this very moment.

I AM
NUMBER 8

CHAPTER ONE

Who *Is* a Number 8?

I wasn't the coolest kid in school. I didn't have the best clothes all the time. Instead of taking me to a barbershop, my mom would cut my hair to save money. And I was terribly awkward when it came to speaking to girls. Guys made fun of me because of my discount store clothes, lack of a cool haircut, and buckteeth. Add to all of this a diagnosis of alopecia and you have the perfect recipe for long-term virginity. I was always picked last to play sports on the playground. Seriously! Didn't matter what sport it was—basketball, football, or baseball—nobody wanted me on their team. I threw like a girl. Wait, scratch that! There are some amazing women softball players. I threw like someone who had no clue where the ball was actually supposed to go. It wasn't until I had failed repeatedly to make the baseball team that I found out why I threw this way. I was left-handed but my mom had bought me a right-hand glove. Thanks, Mom!

I maybe had two "fights" in my whole school career—and I lost them both. A younger kid named Myron threw rocks at my bike once and I told him to stop. He didn't, so I walked over to him across the brown mounds of dirt on the baseball field like I was really going to do something about it. He hit me right in the eye. I immediately said, "I quit."

It might be a little funny now but I also remember the feelings of isolation that came from this constant ridicule. Not to mention that I was *always* at church. My mother kept me in the choir, Boy Scouts, and probably every church play ever written. So, in sum, I was the corny, virginal, bucktoothed church boy. I can't even count how many times, when everyone else was out partying, I was at home with my mama. She said I couldn't do what everyone else did. She said I had a calling on my life. It didn't always feel that way though. When I was younger, I hated this calling Mama said I had. It made my life so lonely.

I was a number 8.

Called by God: A Game Changer

Do you remember the moment that was the game changer for you? You know, when that person or event showed you that things would not be the same? Maybe after years of losing, you finally won the big game—exactly at the moment when people who could offer you a college education or a professional contract were watching.

Maybe after struggling with your voice forever, you finally sang a solo and nailed it in front of the entire school. Or maybe after a million and one false starts, you finally launched your new business. It could be that you have been sick for a long time and, at last, you receive a new diagnosis that you are now "cancer-free."

These are all game changers! Moments that turn the tide for you and help you believe something entirely different about yourself. It is when you know you are stronger than you thought, more brave than you knew, and that you have a bigger purpose than you believed.

These moments don't necessarily mean you will look different or that other people won't see the same person and continue to ignore, dismiss, or try to keep you down. But what is important is that something has changed in you. You know that—in spite of appearances—your heart has changed. You know that you are in the will of God and nothing can stop you from having your dream.

Our David had a game-changing moment. Remember, in the early part of his life, he'd spent hours in the fields watching sheep. His typical day was: Wake up while it was still dark, get the sheep from where they slept (the sheepfold); walk and walk and walk until he found water for the sheep; sit while the sheep ate and slept; guard the sheep against bears, lions, and humans that might harm them;

gather the sheep from where they wandered around—they didn't know where they were going—and then walk the sheep back to the sheepfold. And that was a good day. Not exactly a party.

Take a minute and imagine living the life of a shepherd: You smell that? Chasing sheep in a field means that your feet would likely be covered in the fetid remnants of the day's grazing. And how about that Middle Eastern heat? Can you imagine the sweat pouring off your face? It would certainly sting your eyes. Feel the rays of the sun beating down on you like you're the only person in the world. Your only respite is an occasional breeze. But those fleeting moments of relief give way to the inescapable reality that this is your life. A life relegated to the shadows.

On the really hard days, David, as all shepherds do, had to rescue a sheep by fighting a wild animal (see 1 Sam. 17: 34–35). Or, he had to spend all night either searching for one or sleeping in the sheepfold. Do you see where I'm going with this? Being a shepherd was hard work, but somebody had to do it. That somebody, during David's time, was usually the youngest son. David was the youngest son.

To say that David's days were busy does not do him justice. But even with fighting wild animals, chasing sheep up and down mountains, and walking for miles, David still had time for his music. In fact, he had hours and hours of time to play, sing, and even write his own songs. So, even though David was doing the work for his father, he still had time to do the work God called him to do: praise God with his music. We enjoy them now as the Psalms, but David wrote some of those inspiring verses from his experiences while watching sheep.

But it was a thankless job, being a shepherd. No advancement. No raises. Not much acknowledgment. No prestige. Just a thankless job given to the younger sons, who often would not inherit land like the older ones. I also imagine that because babies of the family were often considered a nuisance, it's believed that shepherding was a way to occupy their time accordingly.

Therefore, we can assume that Jesse, David's father, knew what he was doing. And he knew whom he was doing it to. It was the tradition. David was the youngest and, most likely, the one that got the least attention. Yet there was something beneath layers of dirt, crud, and tall stories he always seemed ready to share. I envision Jesse dismissing David in the absentminded way parents do sometimes. "Yes, son, you killed a bear today. Really? You killed a lion too? Uh-huh. That's very good, son. Go sit over there."

I also imagine that when David heard that Jesse was calling him in from the field, in the middle of the day, he was a little afraid. It's like someone coming up to your school or on your job—"Hey, we need to see you. We need you to come with us." I know what that feeling is like: "Me? You talking to me? What? What's going on?" At the same time I know I'm thinking, "Am I in trouble?"

David was being called in. The game was about to change. Samuel, the prophet of God, had been sent to ordain one of Jesse's sons. After receiving the mandate from Yahweh, Samuel just got on the road. He didn't say "Which one God? Give me some details." In fact, he was more afraid of the current king, Saul, finding out (see 1 Sam. 16:2). But he went. And Jesse lined up his sons. Surely these tall, accomplished sons were the ones Samuel wanted to see. Jesse was proud of his sons who worked beside him on the farm, sons who were tall and strong and could sit at the table with their father and speak his language. Out of these seven sons, one of them must be king, right?

Samuel was prepared to anoint the firstborn. Tradition told him that the firstborn received the inheritance. God wasn't having it. Samuel went to the next one and the next one, and then stood at the last son in the room. None of them were the one (see 1 Sam. 16:6–10).

Then Samuel asked, "Are these all the sons you have?" (1 Sam. 16:11).

Jesse brought him seven sons, but God knew there was yet one left. God told Samuel to wait for the son who was overlooked, the one out in "left field," the one who nobody expected to be or do anything other than guard the sheep and sing and play his music. God told Samuel to anoint the eighth son because God wasn't looking at David as a shepherd, dirty, talking to himself, and different from the other sons. God wasn't looking at what the world thought a great person should look like. God was looking at what was inside his heart: courage, faith, and the desire to please God. Our all-knowing, all-seeing God was looking for someone after His own heart. Someone born to lead. Someone born to be royalty. Someone just like you.

So David leaves the sheep to see what is happening. He doesn't know it yet but he is about to experience that game-changing moment I spoke of earlier. David is about to walk into his destiny. He is to be anointed king. God has selected David, the shepherd, the one who sits with *sheep* all day and all night, the one who is forgotten when it's time for blessings to be given. The one whose own father overlooks, ignores, leaves him out. David stayed in the background. Tradition said he had to. But God isn't bound to adhere to man's tradition. I imagine his brothers and father were standing there with their mouths open. What could God possibly want with an eighth son?

When God calls you, the game changes.

Many of our stories are not very different from David's. In fact, given the isolation I experienced in my childhood, I would have probably been a shepherd too. Oh yeah, except it was the 1970s and no one I knew spent their days and nights watching sheep. Nevertheless, I might as well have been in the pasture because I was certainly in the background.

Who Is a Number 8?

In biblical numerology, the number seven is the symbol of completion, of divine perfection. Joshua marched around

Jericho seven times, seven priests blew seven trumpets to complete the destruction of Jericho (see Josh. 6). Naaman was told to bathe in the Jordan seven times to be completely cleansed of his leprosy (see 2 Kings 5:10). Oh but the number 8? That's the number of new beginnings. David represented a new beginning for his family, for the nation, and for how God would interact with His people and choose their leaders. Jesse had seven sons standing before Samuel, which would lead us to believe that Jesse felt complete and satisfied with these sons. But, wait—Jesse has eight sons. So what does that mean?

I think it means that if we look at the first part of David's story with our oft-faulty human eyes we could say that being a number 8 is one too many. A number 8 is unwanted and forgotten. But through the eyes of God, being a number 8 is cause for celebration. David's story reveals to us that number 8s have a God-ordained future. Number 8s are special because God created them for His purpose. You may not have known you were a number 8, but you may have known you were not like everyone else. Your mama and daddy may not understand you. Your sisters and brothers, classmates, coworkers, church members, friends, children, partner may have thought or said, "Oh, you know John, he's, well, he's *different*."

Well get ready to shout! When you read about what it means to be a number 8 in these pages—through the lens of David's life and my own—there will be nothing left for you to do but rejoice. Sure, you will recognize the hurts, the tears, and the times you felt like you were keeping the sheep. But you will also see yourself in the strengths, the willingness to keep going, the inside fire that says, "I will do this!"

But before we dig in any further, before we unearth the painful places, I want to give you upfront the twelve strengths that, as a number 8, will help you fulfill the special purpose planted in you by God despite your trials. If you have been anointed a number 8, you will see yourself in the following. Number 8s:

1. Celebrate the successes of others as well as their own: Number 8s humbly recognize that it is God's pleasure for all of us to flourish.

2. Are eager to learn: Number 8s don't seek the spotlight but are prepared for it when it happens.

3. Are willing to wait: Number 8s often exist on the fringes, barely making impact, until suddenly they are chosen and everything changes. Number 8s develop an indomitable patience because of the amount and depth of waiting they have to do.

4. Keep going: Number 8s are warriors who are not willing to let "no" keep them from their destiny. They are persistent.

5. Trust God: Number 8s are able to actualize their full potential because they have faith that God is fighting their battles.

6. Practice prayer and praise: Number 8s, like David, have learned the secret to sanity in an unstable

time—prayer and praise. Worshipping God removes fear.

7. Learn from failure: Number 8s know that failure is not forever. Failure is often an opportunity to learn what does work.

8. Care for our temple: Number 8s show discipline by taking care of their body, mind, and spirit. As God lifts them higher they know they need to be well to be their best.

9. Balance loving God with loving others: Number 8s fight to maintain *balance* between personal relationships and the call of God on their lives.

10. Have a heart for God: Number 8s search for a fatherly stamp of approval; whether it's their earthly father or heavenly Father, they want to make Dad proud.

11. Live with passion: Number 8s are passionate about their purpose and fight for justice.

12. Were born royalty: Numbers 8s aren't what they look like. Underneath the "swaddling clothes" (the shyness, the differences) lies a king or queen that God has called to a great *destiny*.

You may not be able to see all of these in yourself right now. You may not even know what your purpose is today, but when you recognize that you are a number 8, when you can say "Yes, this sounds like me" or "Yes, this is me," you have already begun the journey toward God's call. You're not invisible. God sees you and is calling you in from the fields so you can receive your anointing.

———————

Questions for Reflection

1. Do you identify yourself as a number 8 based on the description in the chapter? Why or why not?
2. Is there a particular strength that resonates with you from this list? Which one and why?
3. Have you had a game-changing moment? If so, what was it and what shift did it create in your life?

CHAPTER TWO

The Field of Favor

For many years, I wanted to be a singer and actor. I just knew I had the gift. People were always telling me I was talented. "You should go to L.A." "You should try to do sitcoms." "Have you ever thought about doing stand-up?" "You should try the *Laugh Factory* or the *Funny Bone*." But for whatever reason, I never felt like that was the direction I was supposed to go in. That wasn't for me. People were like, "You should hone your comedic gift," and I was thinking to myself, "I honed my gift trying to get out of spankings from my mama." I knew that if I could make her laugh, I wasn't going to get in trouble as much. So, in a way, I groomed my gift out of a need for survival and to avoid pain.

But, for a time, I bought into what people were saying.

I tried things. I did comedy. I recorded albums. I started companies. I was feeling my way around, trying to find my worth and value in these things. Ed Steele at EdSteele Worship.com says this about how we process our worth and value:

> Misplaced understanding of our self-worth is another reason that some resist confession of guilt. When self-worth is based on our perceived performance, failure to perform adequately destroys the image we see and measure ourselves by and we will do almost anything for the self-preservation of who we think we are, or believe that others think we are. The truth is that our worth comes from what Jesus Christ has done for us, not from what we might be able to do. That's part of the beauty of God's grace.

I had to stop trying to find my worth in what I did for God and start living for God, Who'd already called me His. This resonates with something that I once heard Dr. James Morman say that stayed with me for the rest of my life. He said, "Anything rare is inherently valuable."

See, there's no shortage of CEOs and comedians and singers. And truthfully, there's nothing inherently wrong with any of those paths. But there does seem to be a severe lack of principled, committed, humble, integrity-filled leaders. Men and women who have been broken, not just for the sake of brokenness, but so that they will have a heart for those they serve and those who are coming behind them. And that breaking process comes with time. Times where it will feel like no one gets what you are trying to do. This is exactly why all of my efforts to follow what people said I should be doing fell short.

What God wanted to do with me was rare. That's why it took so long. It's just that way for us number 8s, I suppose. I'm living in a season of favor right now that I tried to access nearly twenty years ago. But God didn't want me doing what I do now back then.

Of course, it didn't change the fact that I knew God had something great for me to do. I always thought I was going to be on TV. I knew I was going to sing. I was sure I'd do a record or ten. I had all of these things in my heart. But when I tried to do them on my own and in my own power, I might have gotten a few opportunities here and there, but it was never the big "king" moment I thought it would become. The truth is, talent wasn't my issue. I had plenty of that. Character was my issue. Maturity was my issue. Vision was my issue. And these are all traits that had to be cultivated by God in my own personal desert place. It took laboring in painful isolation where I was unseen and misunderstood to develop into the person God could use for His purpose—not mine.

How many stories do we have of entertainers and people of great notoriety who, because of their gifts and talents, have ascended to great heights of visibility, but once they arrive, they find themselves completely empty? They search for value and validation at the end of a bottle, or at the end of a puff of smoke, or after an exchange of intimacy with someone they barely know, but none of this can fill the hole in their souls. These are likely people who left the field too soon. They didn't wait for the call. They may not have even been anointed.

Dr. Tim and Theresa Early in an article on David's threefold anointing discusses this:

> Whenever the Lord is to anoint you for service in the administration of HIS kingdom, it is not exclusive to gifting [charismata] alone, but is smeared upon our character and manhood before ministry as well. Surely, it is a delicate process that encompasses much more than the visibility of being in the work of the ministry [For some, it is public success versus private failure], but with the compositional and [spiritual] chemical changes within us for maximum yield in the steadfast counsel [Prov. 8:14] of God.

Like David in the Field

Check this scenario: Bethlehem. A hopeful father. Ambitious sons. An open field. A young boy. Scattered sheep.

As I've noted, David was the last in the line of sons born to Jesse of Bethlehem. As the eighth son, he held the least

amount of esteem in the eyes of his brothers and father.
Tradition dictated that Jesse relegate his youngest boy to
the fields to watch a few sheep. But what looked like a field
for the forgotten was actually a field of favor, where the
foundation was laid for a boy who would be king.

God told Samuel to come to Bethlehem. He told him
there was a king in Bethlehem. He told him there was a
king in Jesse's house. But it wasn't one of the seven. It was
number 8. It was David: the mistake.

What?!

Yes, Jewish historians believe that David was conceived
from a very complicated and seemingly adulterous relationship. Thank God things aren't always what they seem,
right? Author Jeremy Meyers explains David's backstory on
his blog, Redeeming God:

David's father, Jesse, was the son of Obed, who was
the son of Boaz, who married Ruth, the Moabite
woman. The Jewish traditional law explicitly forbade
Hebrew women from marrying Moabite men because
of how the Moabites treated the Israelites when they
were wandering in the desert after fleeing Egypt. But
the law was unclear about whether or not a Hebrew
man could marry a Moabite woman. Boaz believed
that the law allowed such a marriage, which is why he
married Ruth.

However, according to Jewish tradition, Boaz
died on the night that he and Ruth were married

(Midrash, Zuta, Ruth 4). Many believed that his death proved that God had condemned Boaz' marriage to Ruth, and had punished him accordingly.

However, even though Boaz and Ruth had only been intimate for that one night, she conceived and gave birth to Obed.

Obed was then viewed as illegitimately born, as was his own son, Jesse. Nevertheless, both of these men labored hard in learning the Torah and loving God and so the conduct of their lives helped convince the surrounding communities that they were accepted by God.

After Jesse had been married to a Jewish girl named Nizbeth (Babylonian Talmud, Baba Batra 91a) for many years and had fathered seven sons with Nizbeth...doubts began to fill his mind about whether or not his line and seed were permanently polluted by his Moabite blood. It was at this point that he resolved to cease all sexual relations with Nizbeth. He did this out of love for her, because she, as a pure Israelite, would be sinning to be married to someone who was of impure Moabite ancestry.

So Jesse, wanting a legitimate heir, came up with a plan to have a son in the same way that his forefather Abraham had done: through relations with his wife's Canaanite maidservant. Whether Jesse was viewed by God as a true Israelite or just as a Moabite convert to Judaism, the law allowed him to marry a female convert to Judaism. If he obtained a son from this union, this son would be recognized by all as a legitimate heir, thus securing Jesse's family line.

When the Canaanite woman was told of this plan, she did not want to participate, for she loved Nizbeth, and had seen the pain that she had gone through by being separated from her husband for so many years. So she told Nizbeth about Jesse's plan, and the two of them decided to do what Laban had done so many years earlier with Leah and Rachel. So on the night that Jesse was to have relations with the Canaanite maidservant, she switched places with her Nizbeth. On that night, Nizbeth conceived, and Jesse remained ignorant of what had taken place.

But several months later, Nizbeth began to show that she was with child, and her seven sons, as well as her husband, all believed that she had committed adultery. The sons wanted to kill their adulterous mother by stoning (as the law called for) and her illegitimate baby with her, but out of love for his wife, Jesse intervened. Nizbeth did not reveal to her husband that the child was his, for she did not want to embarrass him by revealing the truth of what had happened. Instead, she chose to bear the shame of their son, much as her ancestress Tamar was prepared to be burned rather than bring public shame upon Judah, her father-in-law and the father of her child (Gen. 38:24–25).

Oh the things we do when we operate out of our own flesh! If Jesse believed that David was the product of an adulterous relationship then this would constitute an embarrassing secret. It would make sense then that Jesse would keep this "mistake" hidden in the field.

But God, through Samuel, had called this mistake in from the cold. David was being called in from the field.

Isn't it amazing that we actually see a foreshadowing of Jesus here? When Mary gave birth to Jesus, many people thought He was the product of an adulterous affair she'd had prior to marrying Joseph. Like Jesse intervening in Nizbeth's life, Joseph intervened on behalf of Mary. Both women would have been stoned according to Jewish law. Both women were carrying a king.

God is a redeemer of broken situations. He can bring value out of our most shameful seasons. He specializes in giving us beauty for our ashes. God's sovereign will mandates that there is no such thing as an accidental life. All life is a direct result of the voice of God. You cannot sneak into the earth, you must be spoken into it. David, though an inconvenient truth for his parents, was a declared son in the eyes of God. And relegated to field duty, he was content to do whatever his dad asked him to do. Despite tradition, despite the circumstances of his birth, despite the possibility of being disliked and shamed, David remained honorable. His circumstances required honor, deference, humility, hard work, and acts of service. This was the beginning of his field training.

While a prophetic drama was unfolding in his house, and before he was called, David was in the field. Writing songs. Praying to God. Sharing his heart. I imagine that there were days when David hated that field. It symbolized rejection. It symbolized a lack of value. It was the place that reminded him of his outsider status. It seemed like he was always going to be a shepherd despite what he felt in his heart. After some years, I suspect that David was probably resigned to his station in life.

And how exactly does one handle the realization that the only horizon he or she will see is the rolling meadows of his or her childhood? There was nobody to talk to, so David would talk to God. When the sky is all you have, it becomes your canvas. David would paint the sky with prayers, poems, and praise songs that had angels leaning in from the edges of Heaven to listen.

There was no way that David could know that the field he once despised was now the field he needed to survive. The field became the place of his deepest expression. It was the place where David could share his heart uninterrupted. He didn't have to fight with seven other voices for attention. In the field, he began lifelong communion with the Living God. God was all he had, and he soon learned that God was all he needed.

But it wasn't just a love fest out there. He would occasionally be interrupted with work.

David would be writing a song and see a lion in the distance with one of his sheep in its grasp. David would simultaneously kill it while making sure the sheep was okay. Once the crisis was averted, he would likely go back to writing. Or singing. Or dancing. As he'd start on another song, maybe a bear would come along. He would kill it, check on the condition of the sheep, and go back to writing. The work never stopped, but neither did the preparation.

This is the journey of a number 8.

Your Field of Favor

For many of us, the moments in life where we feel most isolated can cause us to feel like God has forgotten us. But the repetition and isolation are actually developing our sensitivity to God's voice and giving us strength to stand on our own when it's our time to lead.

It's in the isolation of the field that God creates the greatest leaders. The utter intensity of aloneness is the fertile ground for the birthing of creativity. The field is a sacred place where the hearts of men connect to the sounds of heaven.

Here's another hard truth: A broken heart is easily tuned to the frequency of God. David had found this secret. Among the sounds of bleating sheep, the whisper of passing winds, and the breaking of his own heart, David learned to discern the voice of the living God.

The intimacy David established with God in the field would prove invaluable throughout the rest of his life.

Nothing settles your heart like knowing you're loved. David discovered that the rejection of man was the acceptance of God. There were no crowds in the field, so he didn't write for them. He wrote his songs for an audience of One. Yes, alone in a field was a boy who would become a man; a man who would become a king. But none of that was his goal. He just wanted to sing songs that would make his heavenly Father smile.

I remember my first foray into songwriting. I would stare out the window of our tiny apartment in Cincinnati and sing songs I'd made up to God. I don't know how they sounded or if anyone was even listening when the window was open. It didn't matter what anyone thought. I wasn't singing to them. Somehow I knew God heard me. My songs, at that time, weren't written for the crowd.

Number 8s don't care too much for crowds. We don't mind the crowds, but we don't live for them either. Developed in anonymous fields, number 8s rise from every section of society. From every field of endeavor, we come. Often misunderstood, mostly relegated to menial tasks, and too many times marginalized, number 8s don't force our way to the front. What usually happens is, suddenly, without warning, we are needed. Like Samuel looking for God's anointed king, we are called out without notice. But because of our time in the field, when called upon, we have the strength, courage, and heart to ignite a team, a city, or a nation. For those of us who ever felt overlooked and lightly regarded, the field of anonymity was the place where our honor was seeded, our intimacy with God was established, and our leadership skills birthed.

It is entirely possible that we would have never heard of the great King David, the great warrior of the battlefield, if young David had not been anonymous in the shepherd's field. Anonymity is the cloak God uses to develop, foster, prune, and then ultimately produce greatness. Sure, anonymity hurts when you know you have a gift. Being overlooked stings when you see others whose gifts mirror your own looking like they're achieving great success. But take heart, friends! God knows exactly what He's doing. He knows exactly who you are. He knows exactly where you are. And He is saving you for an appointed time, a specific moment to unveil you.

Scripture says in Rom. 8:18–19 the following:

> For I consider that the sufferings of this present time are not worthy *to be compared* with the glory which shall be revealed in us. For the earnest expectation of the creation eagerly waits for the revealing of the sons of God.

Ah, the sons (and daughters) of God! The earth is waiting for those who have yet to take the stage, in every area of necessity. But before we take the stage, in any area, it's critical that we don't rush past the beauty of our fields. There's favor there. Not favor like we tend to think of it in our consumerist culture: houses, cars, etc. This favored place is where God grooms, plants, prunes, and ultimately produces and develops you for the thing you were called and assigned to do.

And it's not always an easy place to live.

Honestly, it's hard even for me to write this because, by nature, I'm inherently impatient. I don't like to wait for anything. I'm a part of Generation X, the microwave generation. If I could microwave thanksgiving dinner, I probably would. And we Gen X'rs have given birth to the Internet generation: millennials, who seems to move at the speed of light. But the truth is, you can't microwave spirituality. You can't click a computer key twice and produce spiritual maturity.

I love God, but I admit there are times when I find myself complaining that He takes too long. There are times when I feel like I'm ready to do or say something as soon as I feel it, as soon as I sense it, but it's not time. I've had to learn that God will put the seed of something in your heart and then process you for years before that thing becomes reality. But aren't we all like this sometimes? We're like, "God, come on. Let's build it. Let's go!" And God's saying, "I am building it. I am building it." And we're like, "But I don't see it! I don't see it!" He's like, "Because it's hidden beneath the surface."

To Be Hidden

The highest structures often have the deepest foundations. Many people want to ascend to the highest places of authority and position, but they neglect to understand that those positions come with a certain level of requisite responsibility and humility, and if you don't go through the foundational places, if you don't allow God to dig deep into your life, you will set yourself up to become a tyrant. You will be a talented, gifted individual who doesn't have empathy or passion for those who are connected to you. Those are the worst kinds of leaders.

The field is where God proves your character. The field is where God deals with your heart. The field is where He takes you through the challenges of being innocuous, invisible, unseen, and delegated mundane daily rituals. Whether we know it or not, all of this is producing in us a level of staying power that we would not have if we'd gotten our portion easy.

It's God's love that keeps us safe in the field. As a shepherd, David didn't have human interaction on a day-to-day basis. He didn't have people to bounce things off of or to help him process things. He literally had to be faithful to sheep. And I'm certain there were times when he'd talk to those sheep. Poor David, he probably thought he was going crazy. He probably named the sheep. "Hey, Tasha! Come back here!" "Joe, leave Shauna and her babies alone!" I know that sounds funny, but it was exactly what God wanted to do in David. God wanted David to become so committed to something that other people thought had so little value that he would literally put his life on the line for it. On the surface, it seemed insane. What could God possibly be doing in David's life that needed him to sit out in a field, lonely and talking to sheep? The answer is this: He was grooming David to understand that everybody has value, and no matter how lost or how many bad decisions a "sheep" might make, you fight for them, because they can't fight for themselves. Starting with David toppling the Philistine giant, Goliath (see 1 Sam. 17), and continuing with him leading the great army of Israel, God made a general out of a shepherd following and caring for sheep.

What qualified David to face Goliath and other armies was his faithfulness in the field. What's going to qualify you for the place of prominence and position that I believe God wants you to occupy will be your ability to remain faithful in the areas that seem insignificant now. I can guarantee you, I can assure you, what looks insignificant now will have great residual benefits in the years to come. And not just for you, but for anyone that's connected to you, whether that's a spouse, children, grandchildren, or anyone else in your sphere of influence.

Everybody's process is different. Everyone's timing is different. Remember my dream of being a singer? I'd been singing since I was a little boy. But only now am I coming into a place where I believe my voice is something that the masses need to connect to. I've done records before, but it wasn't time for the world to hear me. See, every voice has a texture. Every life has a tone. What is the tone of your life, fellow number 8? How does that tone align with the times?

If you have the right tone for the times, then God will tune you to a generation. But only when it's time to do so. This generation needs uncompromising voices and committed leaders who are unashamed of their faith, unashamed of their principles, unashamed of what they stand for. And all of that is honed in the field. David made no qualms when speaking to King Saul about going after Goliath. He said, "I killed a lion and a bear in my dad's field and I'm going to kill this Goliath who disrespects the God that I serve" (see 1 Sam. 17:36). That wasn't David's home training talking. That was his field training talking.

Did you know that the field has been training you for such a time as this? The places of loneliness, isolation, and misunderstanding have been preparing you for this moment. People don't even know they need you, but they're about to find out how badly they do. So this is the season to remain humble and committed and work just as hard as you've ever worked. This is the time to be so profoundly impacted by God's process that you don't need external validation. David didn't need anyone to tell him he was a warrior. He knew it. And I'm here to tell you that, as a number 8, you are a warrior too! You are a winner! You are a leader! Make peace with the field. It's a field of favor. When you do, and God calls your name, that peace will overtake you. Make peace with the process and you'll also have peace that whatever is coming down the road, you are equipped to handle it.

Questions for Reflection

1. What was your field of favor? How did you come to recognize it as such?
2. What does one do while in a field of favor? Consider David's actions as a model.
3. How is one's ability to hear God refined in the field of favor?

CHAPTER THREE

There's Oil in the Field

It wasn't a shepherd's field but it might as well have been. I'd just come home from college and was working at a day care center. In fact, it was the very same center where my mother used to drop me off when I was a little boy. While working there as a teacher's assistant, I also worked at a pharmacy. I would love to say that I was just on summer break and trying to make some extra money before returning to school, but that would be a lie. I'd flunked out of college. And at twenty years old, I was trying to make ends meet as I figured my life out.

I had no idea what direction to take, where to go. I had much potential, but very little vision. Yet I was blessed in that season to have the stability of a mother who loved me and reminded me that God had a plan for my life. She didn't beat me up for not achieving. She discerned that there was something else in me beyond what I was manifesting, and she spoke to that.

When you're in seasons of challenge, brokenness, and failure, identify the voices that will speak not only to your current situation—we all need accountability—but to your future self. Find people who will speak life into where you're going. I didn't need people to tell me what was wrong. I knew what was wrong. And if I could have fixed it, I think I would have. I needed somebody to say what was right. The truth was, I was immature and unwilling to do the hard work necessary to achieve the level of academic success I desired. I lacked critical foundational skills. These were the things that were wrong. But what was right was that my heart was pure. I wanted to serve God and I was willing to do whatever it took to become what He wanted me to be. It wasn't success that gave me that heart either. It was failure.

Sometimes the greatest necessity to success is utter failure. I went to college to try to get a degree so I could have a job. But that was never the highest form of purpose God had for me. I needed to find my passion, and just going through the academic motions was never going to allow me to find and unlock my particular passion. That's the thing about us number 8s. We're passionate folk. We're passionate in our relationships, and in just about everything we do. The problem is, sometimes we misplace that passion. We are passionate about people and things that don't deserve such a high level of commitment.

I met some wonderful people in college, but for me, it would not be the place that could reveal my purpose. My passion was to serve hurting people. I didn't know how to make a career out of that though. At twenty, I didn't know how to identify opportunities for gainful employment that would align with my passion. How do you put "Hey, I want to help people who are hurting" on a résumé? I knew I wasn't supposed to be in the medical field, but I also knew I wanted to do something that facilitated the healing of people's hearts. Yes, I knew I was not called to be some great cardiologist or some type of cardiothoracic surgeon. I wasn't called to fix aortas and ventricles in the physical, but I was certain that I was called to speak to hearts in the spiritual sense.

A couple of years after returning home and working my consistent but mundane jobs, I found myself sitting in the back of Christ Emmanuel Christian Fellowship church. I was nearly twenty-two years old by then. Inside the church bulletin, there was an announcement about a job opening at the City Gospel Mission, a homeless shelter for men in downtown Cincinnati. For some reason, the thought of working at that homeless shelter sparked something in me, something that would change the trajectory of my life.

Growing up, I knew family members, uncles in particular, who by their own choice didn't want to live in a typical community. One uncle was brilliant, but for whatever reason, he wanted to live in his van. He had such a tremendous brain, and while he didn't have the opportunity to go to college, he was a self-taught, do-it-yourself mechanic and electrician. All around the 'hood, people would pay him to fix TVs and all kinds of radios and cars. Again, he had this brilliant brain but didn't really know how to put his life together. He had all these great gifts but still didn't know how to live a regular day-to-day life. And being a young adult at the time, I was terrified that I would become like him. All around me, there were men in my life who were barely getting by, content to do just enough to eat for the day and try to figure it out the next. I didn't want to live that way. I wanted to identify my passion and find a way to unlock whatever other areas of my life would get me to where it was God wanted me to go. Reading that little bulletin was my first step toward that reality.

I went downtown and I applied for the position with a gentleman named Ed. I remember his face like it was yesterday. Ed was tall, wore glasses, and his hair looked much like my hair does now—nonexistent. But he was a good man with kind eyes. He asked me some questions and took me around the facility. He showed me the chapel where they invited both men and women to come in for service. He took me downstairs where they fed as many people as they were able, and then he took me upstairs to see the limited number of beds. There were only thirty, maybe thirty-six, beds and it was first come, first serve. There was always a line for those beds.

Needless to say, I got the job. I don't even remember what it paid because it didn't matter. I wanted to do it. I quit my other two jobs, at the pharmacy and the day care, and moved on to the homeless shelter. I never felt more alive, more in the will of God, than when I worked there serving those men.

I'm often asked how I found myself preaching at Lakewood Church with Pastor Joel Osteen. It was certainly no one but God who "got me here," but I can share where this gift of preaching began to show itself. I believe it started when I was working at that homeless shelter.

There were nights when I got to preach at the shelter's chapel and God would move so mightily. Make no mistake...this was absolutely the moment when the game changed for me. I was still in the shepherd's field. There were no cameras. There were no radios. No one knew who I was. No one was retweeting or Facebook sharing my sermons. I simply preached to homeless men and women about the goodness of Jesus, did my work, and went home. But to see those broken eyes light up, these hopeless souls find their own spark. It got to the point where the chapel was becoming crowded. Homeless people were telling other homeless people, "You need to come hear this guy." And I got the nickname "The Homeless Preacher."

Sometimes at the end of my sermon, I would see crack pipes, bags of weed, needles, and condoms on the altar. The men and women would hug me, and yes they smelled like they'd been out in the summer sun all day, but I embraced them because I saw their humanity. I saw their love. And I saw the love of God for me in them. I saw that they were created by the same God who made me. And, I found my passion. I wanted to help people, and I wanted to preach with reckless abandon. Like David writing and singing his songs in anonymity, it didn't matter that no one knew me when I was at the City Gospel Mission. God was watching me. I was in that field faithful, serving people—sheep, if you will—that others thought had no value. God was watching to see how I would treat them. Sure, He always had opportunities like Lakewood in mind for me. But what could happen later in my life was contingent upon my obedience, my understanding, and the commitment to the betterment of the people that were right there in front of me. I never looked at serving at the City Gospel Mission as a stepping-stone to anything else. In fact, I loved it so much, that I would still be there at this very moment if the Lord had not called me out.

It's not in the public view that God develops leaders. It's on the backside of the mountain, like David. It's in the back cubicle of some office. It's in a small town. Maybe a small college or a smaller church. That kid at the lunch table who may not have the best clothes, she's the one who will become the most celebrated fashion designer of this century. These are the people who will emerge as being the most significant contributors to our world.

Because I spent that time in the field of that homeless shelter, on the fringes, God eventually called me—almost literally. One day while I was working at the shelter I got a phone call from a friend of mine who asked me if I was interested in auditioning for a touring stage play. She had just come off tour with a director who was looking for a particular type of individual, and for whatever reason, my name came to her mind. I still don't know how my name came up. I don't know how she got my number. She called and she said, "You need to talk to this director." And I called and David Talbert answered the phone. We had a great conversation and I did a mini-audition right here on the phone.

Then he asked me to send a head shot and a résumé. "Uh, OK," I thought. I had one black-and-white photo and no résumé. So I wrote in marker on a piece of paper, "If you give me a chance, I won't let you down." That was my résumé. And I sent my one head shot. In turn, he sent me a plane ticket to audition.

I struggled with whether or not even to take the opportunity. It was a risk, for sure. I had a sure thing at the homeless shelter, but it was going to require another level of faith to jump out there. There were no guarantees—it was just an audition. But I felt impressed in my spirit that this was the door God was opening for all the other things that He wanted to do. So I packed up way too many articles of clothing, got on a plane to Dallas, Texas, and I never looked back.

So now I was touring with a stage play featuring Kirk Franklin. The next year, I was on tour with him. By twenty-three, I was traveling the world singing and doing comedy—doing all the things I would have done for free but was now getting paid for. God took me from a homeless shelter in Cincinnati to working with the most successful Gospel artist in recording history. Only He could have done that. According to every indicator, that kind of leap should not have happened. But I accepted my calling into ministry and spent time in a hidden place that ultimately set me up for all the other machinations that led me to where I am today.

I suppose the bottom line is this: In my personal shepherd's field, I wandered a bit. I felt lost and purposeless for some time. But through a perseverance that only God could have given me, the oil that was under my feet was soon revealed.

Look for the Oil

What looked like a field of failure, a field of futility, a field of the forgotten, became a field of favor for David and for me. The same is true for you. David was anointed before he even heard his name being called. The oil he was covered with by Samuel was symbolic of what God had already purposed. It was the physical evidence of God's will for his life. I was anointed to preach before I stepped foot in that shelter and saw the manifestation of the power of God. Being there, and watching these beautiful men and women surrender their vices to God, was simply oil: evidence of what God had already decreed. The same is true for you. Your anointing is bubbling underneath that loneliness you feel. There's something God is doing with all your sadness and frustration, the degradation and isolation. For number 8s, there's always oil in our fields.

This oil that God uses to anoint us for His purpose exists even in our desolate place. Every morning when David would get up and walk out to greet the sheep, he knew that he was in the field. He may even have known, through his victories over lions and bears, that he had some favor. But it wasn't always as easy for him to understand the depth of the oil—the great anointing—that existed under his feet. We often don't realize it either.

I know, I know. You've been walking the same hallways, sitting in the same cubicle, and falling asleep in the same classrooms. It's hard to see the "oil" in that. But the next time you are inclined to complain, remember what I talked about in the last chapter—the character traits God is perfecting in you. The next time you walk to your desk, or your class, or wherever it is you think is a monotonous, droning, consistent place of mediocrity, please know God never sends greatness to mediocre places for the mediocrity to remain. He doesn't send light where light already is. He sends light to darkness. And just to make sure your lamp doesn't go out, He makes sure there's ample oil for the journey. There's oil in that job field. There's oil in that school field. There's oil in that relationship field. There's oil in whatever place you find yourself in. You may not see it on the surface, but it's there. We have to have faith that it is there, even when we can't readily see it. God keeps the oil hidden sometimes in our life. Mostly because we're what the elders call hardheaded. We are always trying to make something happen for ourselves. But this thing that's happening to you and me, which happened to David so long ago, is not the work of men. This is the work of God.

Using That Oil

Where did David get his oil from? He got his oil from sitting out in that field, being faithful in the mundane tasks. If you want to be a leader, if you want to be a person that builds other people's faith and be used by God, be faithful in the mundane, be faithful in the hidden place. Lots of times people ask me "How did you develop your preaching voice? How did you develop your gift? Did you practice? What books did you study?" And I tell them that my anointing was developed in a homeless shelter. And later as a janitor/youth pastor. Yes, I'd been on tour with Kirk Franklin and The Family. But when I returned home, I learned that God wasn't through pruning me.

I loved serving as a youth pastor in New Jersey. But I didn't make enough doing that to pay the bills. So when my church was looking for a part-time janitor, I picked up that job too. So on some Sundays, I'd preach my heart out and when the people left, I'd be picking up trash, cleaning toilets, mopping floors, and vacuuming the rug. Sometimes

I was at the church until three in the morning. Then I'd drive forty-five minutes home, get up, and do it all over again. And guess what? I wouldn't trade those days for anything in the world.

Those days and nights of being faithful, cleaning the church, preaching Jesus to eight, ten, or twelve teenagers, were some of my most rewarding times. Again, no one really knew me. But God knew me. And He was pleased with me. See, the beauty of one's time in the field is that you become content. Not complacent. There's a difference. I wasn't complacent. I never said I didn't want to do more, nor did I stop trying to do more. But my heart was surrendered. I said, "If you want me to do more, God, I will. But I am grateful for where you have me right now." And that, to me, is the way to use the oil.

David had no clue that God was going to anoint him a king. All he knew was he had to be faithful. And he wasn't even faithful with people. He was faithful with sheep. Some people would argue that this doesn't correlate with him becoming an effective leader of men. To me, it makes perfect sense. If you're willing to lay down your life for sheep, how much more passionate and protective and fatherly will you be for humans, for men and women? David didn't have to fight. All he had to do was be.

When you begin to notice the oil bubbling under your feet in the field, it's important that you stop striving. Stop fighting and pressing. This particular season is not about doing. It's about being. Being the thing God created, being the thing God intended. It's a kind of lathering process that's going to build and develop you. The oil that's supposed to be poured onto your life will be a reflection of the oil that has been developed in your life. It's the secret place that develops you. It's the secret place that prepares you. It's the unseen preparation that gives you a visible anointing.

I often try to picture the house where the prophet poured the oil on David. It makes me think about the moment I was called into ministry. I wonder if David felt like I did. I knew God had chosen me to do something far beyond my limited abilities and relationships and resources. That's what He does, you know. If you're a number 8 He's going to call you into something that exceeds your limitations, lack of relational connections, and limited resources. Ordinarily these things would hamstring your dreams. But not this time. God is preparing to bring you into a place so magnificent that only He can get the credit for.

None Like You

One of the prevailing narratives of my life has been my desire to be a father. Not solely in the biological sense, although I love my children. When I say "father," I also mean "the first of a generation" or "the beginning of something new." As many great preachers as there are today, I'm fairly sure I don't sound like any of them exclusively. I am uniquely who God made me. That's the beauty of us number 8s. We don't have a "father" to our style. We've always been different. It's how God wired us. We often long for a mentor. We long for someone to lead us. We find ourselves sad and frustrated because there's no one who can do it, there's no one who can help us. Let me set you free right now. You couldn't find them because they don't exist.

There are absolutely people who will help you, those who are sent to assist you on your life's journey. But for number 8s, it's usually only up to a point. There was no one like King David before King David. And there's no one who has been where you are going. The vision that you have, that has yet to be enacted, not many people will be able to fathom. You're not going to simply walk a path, you're going to have to chop down trees. You are the epitome of what it means to be a trailblazer. God didn't give you just shoes for your life travels. He gave you an ax. You're going to have to do some cutting. But don't fret! There may not be anyone in front of you, but when you look over your shoulder, there will be plenty others following you.

This is the power of the oil that you carry with you, the oil that resides right there in your field. Right there in the places where God has hidden you. There's oil in your everyday chores. There's oil in your everyday tasks. There's oil in obeying your parents. If you're a young person reading this book and your parents ask you to do chores, I want you to do it with a fervency and an urgency and an excellence that you have never attacked those tasks with before. Why? Because just like David in the field with sheep, and just like me in that homeless shelter, God is developing and monitoring your response to the process. It's in the small things where God trusts you with bigger things (see Matt. 25:23). It would be great if life was like the movies and every problem or conflict could be happily resolved in an hour and a half. But life doesn't work that way. That's not how God develops greatness. It's one step after another, one decision after another, one task after another. And collectively, very small steps prepare you for a flood of favor.

I'm sure that David was dreaming and daydreaming in his field just like you and I tend to do. Many times when I would be feeling sad, or alone, or misunderstood, I would look out the back window of my childhood home, up past the trees and into the stars, and say, "Someday, I'm going to be great. One day, people will know my name. One day, people will see what I carry." I always believed that I was supposed to do something significant. My mother told me many years ago that when I was a little boy, around four or five, I would watch the world news. Not cartoons— the world news. Walter Cronkite and crew. It was during this time that God clearly said to her, "You are raising a world leader." Whew! That had to be some pretty heavy stuff for a single mother whose husband had just left the family. A mother who was now raising a young, black boy on a limited income in a two-bedroom apartment with no air-conditioning. But she never doubted God in this regard. She knew that one day His word would come to pass.

Well, in many ways, that "one day" has begun to show

itself. But, if I'm honest, it doesn't feel the way I thought it might. I used to think there'd be some kind of vindication. That I would feel like shouting, "See! I told you so! You doubted me but in the words of Chris Brown, 'Look at me now!'" But I don't feel that way at all. When God began putting me in the position of my dreams coming true, I was actually at peace. I was thankful. I wasn't jumping up and down, excited. In fact, it was a sober moment. I said, "God, you did it. You brought me to the thing you promised. And you did it in a way where I'm not walking around condescending, looking down at other people, saying, 'I got mine. Now you need to get yours.'" You see, my time in the field burned all that stuff out of me. The process of waiting, the years of serving other people's vision, the years of celebrating other people's success, pruned away my need for validation. At the time, of course, I didn't know that all I was going through was producing oil under my feet, but it was. And when the phone started ringing and opportunities became more frequent, I was faithful in those doors.

What I learned was that the more you commit to the process and the more you trust God for increase in every area of your life, the more God allows the scales to tip in your favor until one day the momentum is so tremendous that there is no going back to the life you knew. You will look back and realize that you are not the same as when you started, on the day you were sent out to the field. Ironically though, while you are brand-new, you are also strangely familiar. It's the dual nature of a number 8. You're altogether something people have never seen, but you're so familiar, they feel like they already know you. It's the gift. It's the gift that comes with submitting to the process.

All those times I thought I was ready for public platforms and certain stages, God said no. So many people want the platform, but they don't want the process. They want the position, but they don't want the pain. God wants somebody who would much rather sit in the shadows, hang out in the back, cheer others on, because those are the people He can trust with platforms. Platforms don't make you, they can only expose you.

God's timing was and is perfect. Don't rush the timing of God to escape loneliness. Don't rush the process of God to escape the mundane. Don't rush the development of God because you see someone else in what looks like success to you. There is a difference between actual success and the perception of success. Success is not defined by numbers. It is not defined by achievement. It is not defined by external validation of the masses. Success for us, as number 8s, is defined by our obedience to the voice of God. And it is in the field, the place where we are simultaneously fruitless, forgotten, and surrounded by some of our most intimate failures, that God allows our oil to multiply. Your failures do not disqualify you from being used by God.

So take heart! Be encouraged! The field was designed with you in mind. God's been watching the entire time, and in a moment you're going to hear your name. The oil is going to reveal itself. David was faithful in the field but then he got a call. "David, come on up to the house. Somebody wants to see you." You are about to intersect destiny and what's beneath your feet; what's been hidden inside you all this time is about to be poured out over your head.

The oil that was poured onto David physically was the second manifestation, because the oil from the outside couldn't compare to the oil that was already produced from the inside. Very often, God announces that which already existed. In Matt. 3, when Jesus was baptized, he came up out of the water. The Bible says the Holy Spirit descended in the form of a dove and alighted upon Him, and a voice from heaven came saying, "This is my beloved son, in whom I'm well pleased." To me, the significance of that is Jesus hadn't done anything yet. For thirty years, he'd existed in relative anonymity, especially for someone whose birth was so supernatural. By twelve years old, He was confounding the top religious minds of His day. But for thirty years, He was just Jesus, Joseph and Mary's boy, the son of the carpenter, preparing until the time for his public announcement. But he already was on the scene. What was announced at his baptism was always innate. The physical anointing of David was inherent; it was already inside. God only announces what's already there.

David started walking toward the house, not knowing that it was the last walk he'd ever take as someone other than a king. Do you know that there's a day coming very soon where what you've always done is going to be rewarded in such a profound way that no one will be able to get the credit, but God? Keep walking, keep serving, and keep praying. Whether you know it, angels are watching. And yes, the enemy is watching too, but he's powerless to stop what's coming. You've prayed in the field too long. You've cried too many tears and sown too many seeds. You've celebrated too many people's success. It's your turn now. It's your walk. From the field to the house. That walk that David took and that you are about to take was a commencement, a graduation. God was conferring upon him the diploma of the anointed because he had walked out a path in the field. The oil on his feet was ready to be seen.

To be honest, there are many days when I still long for my field place. For my time working in the homeless shelter. This is true even though I don't relish some of the things I had to encounter. You couldn't imagine some of the things I've heard, seen, smelled. The stench of a dormitory filled with men who have been in hundred-degree heat for twenty hours is not a longing of anyone, ever. But what I did appreciate was the reality of it all. Real ministry isn't always cut and dry. It isn't always neat and clean—antiseptic. Real ministry gets your hands dirty. That's the nature of the field. I'm sure there are times when David got a little bit of sheep dung on him. And if you do life right, serve people right, there's going to be a little bit of crap you are going to have to take. But all of it is worth it, because people are worth it, your purpose is worth it, and your future is most certainly worth it.

Questions for Reflection

1. Who is the person that will speak life into you when everything around you looks bleak?
2. How have you been able to recognize the "oil" in your life, despite being isolated in the field?
3. What are the ways in which you remind yourself that God has not forgotten you and that you are being prepared for a purpose?

CHAPTER FOUR

In Search of a Hero

I was in the eleventh grade when a gospel stage play featuring one of my favorite Gospel singing groups came to Cincinnati. I was totally captivated by them for many reasons but mostly because their harmonies were unbelievable and their lyrics spoke to me. This was also the first time I'd ever seen an entire African American, faith-based cast in a play. Needless to say, I was blown away by the production. I was particularly overwhelmed because after seeing the show several times, I had an opportunity to meet the cast. I mean, seriously?! You would have thought I'd met the Jackson 5, that's how big a deal this was for me. The play left me so inspired that I determined that this thing that they were doing—singing and acting—was exactly what I wanted to do with my life.

On the last day of the show's run, I decided to tell some of the band how much their gift of music impacted me. I'd seen a few of them packing up and getting on their tour bus so I went on the bus to shake their hands and tell them, once again, how great they were. When I walked onto the bus, I immediately felt my heart drop to my stomach. There they were, musicians, watching a pornographic film on the VCR. I'd come onto the bus to share how their music had set me on fire for God, and they were watching naked women.

I'll never forget that day. I'll never forget how it shook me. At the time, I didn't understand how someone could be so gifted and yet so disconnected from how that gift impacted others. Their gifts as musicians brought me closer to God, but their gift wasn't represented on that bus. That day I learned that sometimes we lift people far above where they deserve.

Admittedly, I was a teenager living in a very sheltered world. My mother, who I think is one of the greatest women of God of her generation, had lived a model life in front of me. She was my primary example when it came to the development of my faith. So it never occurred to me that someone could say they were a believer but not actually live it out. I didn't know that it was possible to play music with such skill, to be able to usher people into God's presence, but you yourself remain on the outside.

This would be a lesson I'd learn over and over again as a young adult. Over and over, I'd meet gospel artists whose music impacted my soul but who were major letdowns character-wise in person. In fact, it eventually got to the point where I didn't want to meet certain artists because I didn't want their humanity to taint what I'd been able to glean from their work. And the same goes with certain preachers I've encountered over the years. Many have been phenomenal communicators, but some have what I call a greenroom mentality.

I've been in quite a few greenrooms in my life. They are the spaces provided to artists and speakers by a theater or television studio where we can "let our hair down" and relax before our performances. Unfortunately, there have been way too many times when the person on the platform or in front of cameras is very different from the person I meet in the greenroom. I can't explain just how deeply this cuts me. I never, ever want to be two people. And lifting these individuals up on some impossible-to-sustain pedestal has often made me afraid that I would become just like them.

I suppose that is one of many unintended consequences of hero worship. When you hold people higher than you should, and they fall, it's easy to believe that your own fall is inevitable. I've found myself saying, "Well, if he can't maintain a commitment to God's word and faithfulness, how in the world am I going to do it?" I think that's why it is important to realize that these callings of ours are not a game. As musicians, we aren't performing music; we are living our music. As pastors, we aren't just preaching to those folks out there. We are preaching to our own hearts.

But it's also critical that we are very careful about who we call a hero. There are real consequences for all of us when we mix our humanity with our faith and our process, that fieldwork, if you will. The impossible standards people put on us are often difficult for anyone to maintain—especially as we are being pruned and developed for our ultimate purpose. And I get it. The world loves a hero. In a culture that mocks the sacred and scoffs at the idea of the divine, a hero is as close as some will come to the concept of deity. To touch greatness, to ascend into the rarefied air of ethereal selflessness, we tend to like our heroes to be not only altruistic in deeds, but attractive as well. It's why we are shocked when someone who, according to society, is average-looking yet excels beyond our expectation. Nevertheless, without God's clear appointment, no man-made hero can ever sustain that position.

True Heroes Are in the Field—Until They Aren't

We've got it all wrong. Today, in the age of celebrity culture, we make heroes out of people who have what we don't have. It's almost a covetous act. Our heroes tend to be strong and beautiful with lots of money and popularity.

However, in reality, it should be in the mundane and the common that we mine the depths and find our heroes. True heroes, like David, are often still in the field. They are waiting to be called out. We should long for heroes that don't look like heroes, in the cultural sense, after all. We should want heroes that remind us that at any moment, with the right circumstance and opportunity we could be them. Why not me? Why not now? Why not us? Heroes have jobs. They have kids to pick up from school. They have bills on auto-pay. Heroes have gas. Yes, that kind of gas. Real heroes remind us of us.

Consider Susan Boyle: The *Britain's Got Talent* contestant was not a cover model when she walked across the stage to audition for the judges. She was a very "regular"-looking woman. The classic definitions of beauty and aesthetics had fled from her robust frame. But even as audience members laughed and whispered as she stood helpless before a mass of hearts that had been trained not to see her, she had a light in her eyes. She was too sheltered to know she was being mocked, and because of her appearance, the audience's expectations were really low.

But then Susan Boyle opened her mouth and the world cried. She was a revelation. Little did we know that years of isolation had actually prepared her for the moment when she would be revealed to the world. Nothing was ever the same. Her first album went on to sell over 8.3 million units in one year, and she instantly became an icon. More importantly, her story was a cautionary reminder for us not to merely look at the outside of a person in order to ascribe value. Her ascendancy to the place God had called her to be was as much an indictment on our culture as anything else. You see, the very best heroes don't scream "I'm a hero! Look over here!" Real heroes whisper. They sneak up on you. And, as in the case of Boyle, you're never the same.

The danger of misidentifying the chosen based on surface trappings is the greatest disservice to God's creative genius. God has never created any regular thing.

Be Careful What You Ask For

Let's go back a bit in our examination of the story of David. In fact, let's go back to a season that predates his time in the shepherd's field and his anointing as the next king of Israel. The people of Israel wanted a hero. The nation that had the living God as their covering and protector wanted to downgrade. They wanted a king—actually demanded it. They wanted someone who would go out before them into battle, because apparently, God was not enough. This was the time of the Judges. And among the Judges, none had the heart of the people like the prophet Samuel.

Now Samuel called the people together to the Lord at Mizpah. And he said to the people of Israel, "Thus says the Lord, the God of Israel, 'I brought up Israel out of Egypt, and I delivered you from the hand of the Egyptians and from the hand of all the kingdoms that were oppressing you.' But today you have rejected your God, who saves you from all your calamities and your distresses, and you have said to him, 'Set a king over us.' Now therefore present yourselves before the Lord by your tribes and by your thousands" (1 Samuel 10:17–19).

They got what they asked for. After lining up all the tribes and narrowing down the families, Samuel anointed Saul as king of Israel. He was an obvious choice to most: handsome and well liked by many. Scripture says Saul stood head and shoulders above the rest of the people. He had the look the people were longing for. But his height no more made him a king than Shaq's height makes him a skyscraper. External characteristics do not make a king. It is the heart of an individual that makes a true leader worth following. Unfortunately, the coronation of Saul represented man's attempts at making a leader. That never works out.

Saul was not a number 8.

The inherent danger in searching for heroes is that heroes come and go. Heroes fall. They make us believe and then turn right around and make us doubt. Well, they are us after all. Samuel, on the other hand, was a leader of leaders. A prophet without equal. But for the most part, we like our heroes young. Samuel, as a Judge in Israel, made the inevitable mistake of getting old. He was Derek Jeter of the

New York Yankees in the last year of his career—museum piece rather than a necessary function of the group. From the early days of applause and rapturous awe, to the smattering of claps reserved for those whose present iteration is no match for the memories of their best days, Samuel was the people's prophet, but he didn't raise up a legacy. The people of Israel told him point-blank, you're old and your sons don't walk in integrity like you. Since we can't return to who you were in your heyday, make us a king. Manufacture us a new hero.

Talk about a bad idea.

On its face, Israel wanting a king seemed a rather innocuous request. Other nations around them had a king. A monarch could be a rallying point for the people. There was nothing wrong with desiring a centralized leader who could be the focus of adoration. Except for one thing. The Living God had already claimed Israel as His own. Who could show more power, more strength, more love, and more grace than God Himself? Could Israel have ever found a better protector, provider, and defender? We know the answer to that. It is a resounding no. But that did not stop them from desiring something less than God.

Even consistent greatness becomes common in the eyes of the broken. Strangely, Israel wanted something less than perfection. God was too high. Israel wanted something it could touch. Something with the possibility of flaws. Israel wanted to coronate and dethrone someone when it pleased them.

Enter Saul.

He was the answer to a prayer Israel should've never prayed. Samuel told Israel they were making a mistake. They did not care. They wanted a king because all the other nations had a king. Israel had God, but they wanted a man. One requires faith. The other requires sight. If you put on the right outfit with enough trinkets anyone can look royal. But true royalty, true leadership, has nothing to do with anything external. It's in the blood. I could wear a military uniform and parade outside of Buckingham Palace in England, saying that I am the king of England, but that won't make it so. My desire to be king does not make me one.

You can read the early chapters of 1 Samuel for yourself to see how the experiment with Saul worked out. It was an epic fail. The idea failed because Israel wanted to replace God. Saul failed because he was Saul. He couldn't change who he was. No matter what people attempt to make you, you are who you are in your character, ideals, and vision. The crowd can never give you vision. They can only execute vision. It requires a leader to declare vision.

But all was not lost. God had a plan in His heart that would change the nation. In fact, it would change all the nations for all time. Insert dramatic music here.

A nation who had a God, wanted a king, and now needed a leader. Saul disobeyed direct orders, and God had had enough (see 1 Sam. 15). Seems like a pretty short leash, but who can argue with the One whose words made the stars? It would seem to the casual observer that God was too hard on ol' King Saul. After all, Saul had no king before him to mentor him. He was green. Why the rush?

Because the destiny of God's people hung in the balance. God needed an obedient vessel.

Sometimes the choices we make don't line up with the plan and purpose of God. In those times, the will of God supersedes the fickle and shortsighted whims of men. Saul was a nice man. A tall man. But he had a small heart. He was a people pleaser instead of a God pleaser.

And that would not do.

So much for Israel's new hero. Back to the proverbial drawing board. But here's the question that comes up the most when sharing this story: Why would God anoint someone like Saul if He knew he was going to fail?

God will often give us what we want in order to show us that what we want and what we need are not always the same. Israel wanted a king. They needed God. What better way to show Israel their need for God then by allowing their choice to fail in front of them? There is no discerning of color without contrast. There is no appreciation of right and wrong without corresponding correction. There is no understanding of value without a competing choice.

God has not, nor will He ever, make us robots. Men and women must choose Him. It's the choice that adds beauty and texture and value to any relationship. I don't remain in my marriage because I have to. I remain because I choose to. I see the options and have come to the conclusion that nothing is better than what I have at home. And I will give no one a chance to show me otherwise. When choice becomes solidified, legacy can begin.

Israel was in trouble. Saul had led the nation down a path that proved to be destructive and had no hope of renewal. God allowed Israel to have her way for a season, but she did not belong to herself. Therefore God, being sovereign, made a decision with eternity in mind. Israel was the nation through which He would bring about salvation for all mankind. He wasn't about to let this ill-formed leadership experiment hinder His ultimate plan.

Samuel was summoned. Saul was rebuked. The kingdom was prophetically taken from his hands. It was time for a new leader. But who could lead a nation? Saul was an obvious choice to the people. But leaders aren't always obvious. In fact, some of the greatest leaders were hidden until circumstances cried out for greatness, and they answered. Leaders, like heroes, aren't always easily spotted. Israel got the obvious leader, but he turned out to be less than heroic. So God formed a search committee consisting of Himself and chose Saul's successor.

The prophet Samuel was told by God to pack his luggage and take his oil. God was taking Samuel king hunting. This time, that search would end in Bethlehem. A coronation was about to take place. The chosen one would go from obscurity to unprecedented fame and influence in a single moment. But whose heart could endure such a swift and dangerous transition? Who could carry the weight of expectation and win the hearts of the people? Who could grow in wisdom and in stature and in favor with God and men? There was one. Only one.

Apparently, there was a number 8 in a field, taking care of sheep, who through tears and frustration and misunderstandings, had been prepared for that exact moment. Alan Redpath, author of *The Making of a Man of God*, made this powerful statement: "David knew that all the question marks of his life were in the hand of God. He knew it was impossible to be in God's hand and in the enemy's hand at the same time. The gloom begins to disappear and fear departs as faith emerges in glorious triumph. This man is rising out of his testing and adversity to learn to put his utter dependence on the Lord."

Number 8s exist on the fringes of the collective consciousness, barely making an impact. That is, until suddenly they are called upon and everything changes. Like Susan Boyle and King David, they patiently wait their turn.

When a Number 8 Emerges

I believe it's a function of the human condition to desire to be more than average. No one wakes up and says, "Hey, I sure can't wait to be regular today." All of us want to believe that there is something inside of us that can transcend limitations. Even the most cynical among us want to believe that somewhere, somehow, we are more than a collection of incongruent circumstances. We want the parts to fit. We desire for life to make sense. We want to be a part of something great. Even if we never acknowledge it publicly, all of us desire, just once, to be the hero. It is in our nature to search for the divine. We aren't so much searching for divinity, because divinity can be an object to some and a concept to others. When I speak of the divine in this instance, I mean the sublime, the transcendent, the implausible form of highest humanity. We want an answer to the question: How great can we be? We attempt to find our answers in the people we uplift.

It may sound weird to say but man-made heroes have it bad. The pressure. The expectation. The unqualified elevation. When men and women attempt to elevate anything or anyone other than the Creator, that thing, that idea, that person, will fall.

In a world that's as broken and hurting as it's ever been, with wars and conflicts all over the globe, civility, honor, humility, sacrifice, and respect seem to have gone the way of the dodo. Daily images of the atrocities of unchecked aggression, competing worldviews, and the need for power invade our airwaves and fiber-optic altars daily. Oh what people will do for power! The intoxicating, sometimes corrupting effect of power is clearly at the heart of most of the issues our world faces. Between our need to be validated and the need to dominate other humans, this world has become a battle royal for every manner of abuse one can imagine.

This is why the earth needs a new type of individual to emerge from the ashes of our fractured times. The earth needs people who are strong enough to lead yet humble enough to defer credit. The earth needs those who will war for the heart of God while fighting to heal the wounded. The earth needs true heroes. The earth needs a number 8 like David. And me. And you. We aren't the obvious choices. But we are God's choices.

There's a moment quickly approaching when the obvious ones will be seated in order to watch the unscheduled rise of a new kind of leader. Across business, arts, entertainment, and academia, a new trend will emerge. Those whose worth was rooted in the external and temporal will begin to see platforms and opportunities go to those who hearts were seasoned for the moment.

This is the season of the overlooked. This is the moment of the marginalized. This is the time of the forgotten ones. For those of us chosen last on the playground to play pickup games, our moment is now. Emerging from the fields, full of grace and a heart that wins allegiance without trying, new heroes are coming.

The number 8s are coming.

Questions for Reflection

1. In what ways have *you* fallen for the kind of hero worship we see today? (Be specific.) What were the consequences of that for you?

2. How have you sensed God calling you out to be a different kind of leader from what's seen today? How does this pressure to walk toward your purpose and destiny impact how you live your life?

CHAPTER FIVE

The Long Walk Home

I've always known I was different. For the longest time though, I could never put my finger on what was different about me. It just seemed like there was always a spotlight over my head. Not in a "hey, look at me!" way, but almost like I could never get away with the things that most people could get away with. If everybody in my class was cutting up, I would be the one the teacher would catch. If there were multiple people talking, it was my name that got called. I would always say, "Why did you call my name? Why didn't you call Jerry? Or Ronald? We were *all* talking." And the teacher would always point at me, and reply, "But I heard you." I didn't understand that God had put something on my life so significant that people didn't even know why they picked on me. I just wanted to get away with some stuff. I wanted to be let off the hook like my friends. Like I imagine it was for David, the road between being isolated and walking fully in my calling seemed long, arduous, and downright scary. But I walked it anyway because I sensed something remarkable waiting in my Father's house.

There's a moment that comes in your life when you just know. It's kind of an awakening. You sense that your life is no longer going to be average. I remember sitting in a Tuesday night revival service at Bethel Baptist Church, my home church in Cincinnati at the time. A pastor named Dr. C. Dexter Wise from Columbus, Ohio, was preaching. I sat in the back in the church because, well, I had no other option. My mother was the church pianist. She could cut me with one glance if I even thought about hanging with the cool teenagers who were outside talking, laughing, eating candy and ice cream. That night, as Dr. Wise began to preach, I felt an overwhelming sense that God's hand was on me. I can't explain it any other way except to say that I was overwhelmed by the presence of God. There, in that small, beautiful Baptist church, I knew with certainty that God was calling me into ministry. "What does that even mean?" I thought. I didn't know what this new revelation would entail but I definitely knew that I was being called.

And trust me, it was not my idea. Nobody but God called me.

There is no thirteen-year-old on the planet who's truly

excited about preaching. First off, it's like the greatest insurance policy for virginity.

"Hey, what's your name, girl?"

"Yeah? Well, my name is John and I'm a preacher. Do you want to get some ice cream or read a Bible?"

Yeah, right! Nobody wants to hang out with that guy. At the time, I'm sure I thought, "Thanks a lot, God." I probably even hoped I was wrong. I remember asking my mom what she thought, and just like the ride or die Christian she is, she said the words I did not want to hear. She said, "I'm going to pray about it."

You should know that I come from a legacy of praying women. My grandmother was a praying woman and got results. My great-grandmother, filled with the spirit of God, got results. And my mama seemed to have a private line to Jesus' heavenly office. This still didn't stop me from hoping that this time she wouldn't hear anything. Or maybe Jesus would just say, "Child, stop playing!" when she asked Him if I was supposed to preach.

Why the resistance? you ask. Surely preaching is a noble profession, right? Of course it is. But unfortunately, I had seen one too many unsavory examples of people who took authority and abused it. Pastors who didn't honor the word and used the pulpit as a bully platform. At a very young age, I knew these actions didn't line up with what I had encountered in Jesus and knew about His life.

Just like David, my heavenly Father had called me out. Yet there I was, beginning my long walk toward the manifestation of that call, and still wrestling with all the possibilities, all the "whys" and "why me's." I'd told God, "I don't want to be like these preachers I've seen." And God said, "And that's why I've called you to be the contrast."

Still, I wanted to be a lawyer, a singer, an actor, anything but a preacher. However, despite all the different challenges I faced; all the disadvantages I had; all the times I was bullied, laughed at, and mocked; all the times I battled my identity and was unsure of my destiny; God still chose me. I was shocked. Like, God, couldn't you choose somebody else? Somebody who has it all together? Somebody who really wants it?

No.

And that was it. I continued walking the long road. I continued pressing my way home. There were still several years between the time I recognized the call to ministry and my time at the homeless shelter. I would be in my field, walking that path a little longer before I toured with Kirk Franklin or became a youth pastor. But I was headed in the right direction. And I was willing to take that walk.

From Here to There

David was just watching the sheep in his father's field. It was a regular day, nothing special about it. Same soup, just reheated. Then suddenly he hears the familiar voice of his father calling him to come in. I imagine he glanced once more in the direction of the sheep and began walking toward the house.

I wonder how long the walk was between where David was in the field and the house. Was it a mile? Three miles? Ten? David didn't know who was in the house waiting on him. There's no way for any of us to know the enormity of what God has planned. The prayer in Ephesians 3:20 speaks to this: "Now to him who is able to do immeasurably more than all we ask or imagine, according to his power that is at work within us." We can't even imagine what's waiting for us when God calls us out of the field. Certainly, David didn't.

David was being called out of the field. He was being called to a place that was familiar. The place he called home. But he still had a bit of a journey left. He had to get from here, his field of preparation, to there, the place where he'd be anointed.

Yet still, there was no way for David to know that this journey would be his last walk as the anonymous one. As he walked I imagine he was running through his mind the reasons why he might have been called. Maybe he worried a little about something he did or didn't do. I also imagine that the angels observed all this, and the Heavens leaned in to see the walk of a boy who would be crowned king of God's people.

Your Walk to Destiny

Sometimes the walk from your "here" to "there" is long and lonely. Like David, you might find yourself thinking about the ones you left behind. The uncertainty of what's before you might leave you filled with anxiety. But just the same as when that shepherd boy arrived and saw the prophet standing there with the container of oil in his hands, everything will soon become clear.

Wait for it. All the fighting of enemies and the lonely cries to the heavens will eventually make sense. It had to be this way. You had to go through it. You had to have that heartbreak. You had to have that loss. You had to feel that pain. Your time in the field combined with the outward anointing coming your way will give you both the human grit and the spiritual power to connect with people at a deeper level. And it's at that point of connection that God will be glorified.

Gone are the days of leaders who've never gone through anything. Gone are the days of those who refuse to be broken. Or the unbroken walking around disillusioned at the rest of us who have gone through things. Not anymore! God's elevating people who understand what it means to be shattered and put back together again. People who can show you the tape on their hearts and say, "It still works. It's got a couple of scars, but I'm still here."

That's what your journey from the field to your calling is all about. Making peace with it all.

I believe that God uses our journey from "here" to "there" to unravel the inborn leader that's already hidden inside of each one of us. We are number 8s! We are designated for use by God for a particular purpose. We don't go through the pain of rejection and marginalization just to suffer in silence. We don't endure hardship just for the sake of a testimony. We walk through the painful places and the broken places because God has made us strong enough to survive it. And He plans to use it in ways that we could never imagine. God doesn't sentence us to pain. He trusts us with it. When God trusts you with pain and grief and tears, it's not just for you. It's most likely for those people you will be connected to once you arrive at the place of your anointing.

We need authentic leaders. We don't need individuals who are living life in a perpetual Halloween. Those who can only exist if they are wearing a mask and keeping true intimacy at a distance. As you are walking from the field to your destiny, you are learning to live a real, raw, relevant, out-loud life. You own your mistakes but you also say, in the midst of it all, God still chose me.

There will come a day when those who have been overlooked and forgotten and marginalized will suddenly be thrust into a place of position and prominence for everyone to see. The passions and talents that were developed in secret will manifest in magnificent ways to those who didn't even know what you carried. It is the gift and legacy of number 8s. Walk toward it!

Questions for Reflection

1. When was the last time you felt like you were walking in anonymity? And what happened to change that?
2. God always sees us, even if you never find yourself on a large stage. How do you wrestle with the idea that some people may not have a global platform but are still significant in the story God is writing about mankind?

CHAPTER SIX

Sheep, Lions, Bears, and Giants

Since I was very young, I've had a heart to protect people from bullies. I was always a bridge builder. Going to North Avondale Elementary School in Cincinnati, Ohio, meant that I lived in a very diverse neighborhood poised for gentrification. While the neighborhood was about 50 percent African American and 50 percent white, I still didn't understand the nuances of race. There were times when I felt a tension I couldn't explain when my mother and I would go certain places. She'd keep me close to her, but as a young boy, we didn't really talk about it that much. It was just our reality. However, on the playground, I was keenly aware of the distinct differences between the way black kids interacted and white kids interacted. And on either side, the kids who weren't vocal, who were what other people thought were weak, would always get picked on.

This sense of protection and affinity for people who couldn't fend for themselves has been a part of my life for a long time. As noted in an earlier chapter, I'm by far not a fighter. But having grown up being bullied, a result of my needing braces and having alopecia, I knew what it felt like to be picked on. It's almost tribal, this need to dominate the person who is perceived to be the weakest. It's instinctive in a way. For whatever reason, whether it is social domination or a need for acceptance from the masses, people bully those who appear vulnerable. They assume that these people won't hit back.

The bullying—against me or someone else—hurt me deeply and for quite a while when I was really young. But over time I became very thick skinned. I learned to use this emerging gift of communication of mine to deflect insults. My mother used to teach me that if someone said something about my shoes then I should respond with, "Yep, you're right. We don't have a lot of money so this is the best we could do." Or if they talked about my teeth, I should respond with "Yeah, I do have a pretty messed-up grill." And it worked! My responses would disarm my bullies. Before I knew it, the people who were trying to make fun of me had no more ammunition.

And that left them wide open.

I'm not proud of it, but I would take my mom's advice much further than she probably would have wanted me to.

When my bullies were disarmed, when they didn't have anything else to say, I would clap back with a scathing insult to defend myself. If they tried to come for my teeth, I would give my mom's response first, and when they grew quiet, I would say, "Yeah, but your forehead is the size of a small country." This was the beginning of my ability to verbally spar with my bullies. It was also the raging warrior in me emerging. More on that a little later.

Writer Crystal McDowell discusses how we should ideally respond to bullies of all kinds:

> Responding in your flesh or carnal nature will be the easiest, yet most unspiritual way of dealing with a bully. Sometimes your past interactions with bullies will make you more defensive and reactive instead of you being thoughtfully proactive in the Spirit. Seeking wisdom from God leaves no lingering regret and plenty of room for grace. Wisdom nurtures a willing heart and an open mind to draw a bully towards a spirit of repentance.

Yeah, I wasn't quite there yet. I don't think it was right to return the insults. But I must admit that I did grow more confident in my ability to stand up for myself. I didn't dread getting on the bus anymore because I knew I could handle myself with the bullies in the backseats. But here's the thing: not everyone could. Not everyone could verbally spar. And it was those people who I had a heart for. As I

grew more confident, I felt impressed to be a kind of protector of the quiet ones, the underdogs.

I remember one young man—I'll just call him Nicholas. He was a redhead, pudgy, and very kind. He was just an
all-around good kid. Some of the kids from our school would
always mess with him, teasing him and such. I knew what
that felt like. While I was often able to use humor and words
when I got older to wiggle my way out of a bully's grasp, this
kid didn't seem to have that ability. One day, when the teasing was especially bad, the protector in me just rose up.

"Yo, you all can't mess with him anymore because he's
my friend!" I said. And surprisingly, they didn't.

Despite my own wrestling with insecurities and low
self-esteem, I stuck up for Nicholas multiple times. I was
determined to protect him because I knew that he could
not fend for himself. I honestly had no idea what I was
doing, but something in me wanted to protect him from
the verbal jabs that he had to endure from a very vicious
peer group.

In today's age of cyber bulling and social media sham-
ing, I shudder to think about what today's kids might have
done to Nicholas. In 1982, kids were certainly mean and
ugly with their words. But now, a person's vitriol can go
viral. Many kids are having a very difficult time recovering
from the global shame they experience. Many have committed suicide because of it. All because they did not have a
bridge builder to stand in the gap for them.

What I did for Nicholas was a glimpse into my future. I

was going to be a bridge builder. I'd always had a heart to build bridges between races and various cultures. I got that from my mom. After she graduated from college with her degree in social work, graduating with honors, she went on to have a very successful career in mental health in the state of Ohio. When I was young, I would always see photos of my mother, the only brown face in a sea of white faces. And I don't know what kind of microaggressions she endured, what kind of racism and privilege she encountered, what kind of concessions she had to make to exist in a world that didn't celebrate black female independence nor Christian ethics and femininity. But what I did see was a beautiful, classy example of someone who was very clear on who she was. Someone who was unwilling to be anything less than who God created her to be—while simultaneously celebrating the gifts of those around her. She was a team builder, and I got my heart to build bridges and teams from her.

In a time where this kind of parenting was not looked highly upon by blacks or whites, my mother pushed me to be open to the amazing variety of people God had created. She was, by far, not ignorant of the inequality and systemic disenfranchisement that existed for people of color. Yet, whether it was the music I listened to, the programming I watched, or the friends I had, she made sure that she pushed me to have diverse experiences. She was committed to that. I didn't understand why when I was little, but I do now. It was my mom's discernment at work. God had spoken to her about me.

This background is why I'm able to speak to almost any race or culture and be received. My mom raised me to be broad in my thinking, to be broad in my relationships, and to be a bridge of understanding for those who don't come from the same place.

I'm a bridge. That's what my life is about. And it started with redheaded Nicholas on a grade school playground. I am a protector of those who can't speak for or protect themselves. I bring people from different backgrounds together to have conversations that produce solutions to some of our society's ills. This is who we are as number 8s.

Saying Yes to Self-sacrifice

David was a shepherd who had to fight off lions and bears (see 1 Sam. 17:34) in order to protect his father's sheep. I realize that there are some who may argue that challenging a lion and a bear for the life of a sheep was a foolish chance to take. But God was testing the character of David. *Will you lay down your life for a sheep, son? Will you risk yourself for an animal who probably put its own self in harm's way? Will you honor your father's flock, even though you had no ownership stake in the sheep? Is the life of a sheep worth losing your life?*

David's answer was "Yes!" He placed extreme value on something that others thought was replaceable and unworthy of endangering themselves for. David fought for what he believed was right. And he did it in a way that caused his name to be etched in history. That's why David was the forerunner of Jesus Christ, the Good Shepherd, who laid down His life for the sheep. Ray Stedman said on his website, RayStedman.com:

David was not only the forerunner and ancestor according to the flesh of the Lord Jesus, but in his reign he was also a picture of Jesus Christ in the millennium. David went through a time when he was rejected, persecuted, hounded and harassed. But in the time of his exile he gathered men around him who became his leaders, his commanders and his generals when he did become king over the land. Thus David was a picture of Christ in his present rejection, forsaken by the world, gathering in secret those who will be his commanders, generals, and captains when he comes to reign in power and glory over the earth. Christ will come to establish his kingdom, to rule and to reign in righteousness as the scripture says, and David is a picture of that, too. As God develops this and brings it to pass we can also see in the present world scene that God is bringing Christ to his throne at last, where he shall reign in righteousness.

Number 8s fight for those who can't fight for themselves. And sometimes for those who can but won't.

Another Kind of Deliverer

David was a kid. A shepherd. The one who wandered in the field caring for and talking to sheep. But what no one saw, what no one could have known, was that David was a warrior.

David was asked to deliver cheese and bread to his brothers who were on the front lines of the battle for the nation of Israel. He arrived and began asking questions out of curiosity. That's when he found out that a rival nation was running its mouth about Israel and the Living God.

One day Jesse said to David, "Take this basket of roasted grain and these ten loaves of bread, and carry them quickly to your brothers. And give these ten cuts of cheese to their captain. See how your brothers are getting along, and bring back a report on how they are doing." David's brothers were with Saul and the Israelite army at the valley of Elah, fighting against the Philistines.

So David left the sheep with another shepherd and set out early the next morning with the gifts, as Jesse had directed him. He arrived at the camp just as the Israelite army was leaving for the battlefield with shouts and battle cries. Soon the Israelite and Philistine forces stood facing each other, army against army. David left his things with the keeper of supplies and hurried out to the ranks to greet his brothers. As he was talking with them, Goliath, the Philistine champion from Gath, came out from the Philistine ranks. Then David heard him shout his usual taunt to the army of Israel (see 1 Samuel 17:12–23).

"Why are you all coming out to fight?" he called. "I am the Philistine champion, but you are only the servants of Saul. Choose one man to come down here and fight me! If he kills me, then we will be your slaves. But if I kill him, you will be our slaves! I defy the armies of Israel today! Send me a man who will fight me!" When Saul and the Israelites heard this, they were terrified and deeply shaken (1 Sam. 17: 8–11).

Saul was terrified, but David was angry. Did he hear this dude correctly? Did this guy really challenge the people of the Lord? David was so enraged that he volunteered to kill the Philistine giant. Now be clear: Goliath was a formidable opponent. He was trained in the art of war. David was a shepherd from the field delivering what amounted to pizza. All odds should have been on Goliath. But when you are a number 8 and you carry the favor of God on your life, you go from being the delivery boy to the deliverer of a nation. What stirred in David was a righteous indignation at the prideful disrespect shown toward the Living God.

People of Conviction

Whether it's me on the playground or David with his Goliath, number 8s don't fight for the sake of fighting. But when it's time to stand up, when it's time to fight, we are more than capable of doing so—especially on behalf of a righteous cause. It's certainly important for number 8s to pick and choose their battles wisely, whether they are fighting on behalf of themselves, someone else, or for a larger social issue. In today's landscape of moral relativism and secular humanism, where everyone has an autonomy to live how they want and do what they want, we find ourselves legislating things that were unthinkable even twenty years ago. It can be very easy for number 8s to be sucked into a sociopolitical war zone in an effort to stand up for someone else or represent their own conviction. But again, it's critical that we as number 8s don't deep dive into every cause. We must be prayerful about our stances and decide fairly early how to approach our role in defending the defenseless. That said, number 8s are very much people of conviction. Once they take a position, it's generally God and God alone that can move them from their post.

There are absolutely certain things that I just won't budge on. I won't budge on the deity of Christ. I won't budge on what I believe about life and family. These are my convictions. I don't force my conviction on anyone else, even though we live in a society that screams autonomy— that is, until you disagree with what's happening in the mainstream. Then folks very much go into heteronomy, where they want to force you to believe what they believe about a particular thing. Here's the thing: I am all for autonomy. But as a number 8, I believe right is right, even if no one else is for it. I believe wrong is wrong, even if everyone is for it.

As a number 8, you have to make a very clear line of demarcation about who you are and what you believe. Self-actualized number 8s know who they are. When we come to realize our purpose in life we become incredibly laser focused. Something clicks on the inside. And it's not that we don't respect other people's opinions or aren't willing to see another viewpoint. It's just that when our convictions rise up in us, it's very difficult to challenge us. When we feel passionate about a thing, you're not going to shut us up. What I believe about life and politics and philosophy, those are not likely to change. Like the laws of physics, the laws of number 8s are pretty set in stone. It's how we are able to persist through the "field" places. It's how we are able to stand strong when the time comes to protect those who may need our help.

And the thing is, number 8s don't apologize for who we are and how God created us. He created us with strong convictions so we can fight strategically for the weakest ones. I don't physically fight people, but I use whatever influence I have to shield others who may not have the same capacity to combat bullying or anything else. Some people are just mentally more fragile. And as a number 8, we tend to be empathic and can tell when someone is in pain, even when that pain doesn't show outwardly. We feel deeply.

I want you to know that the pain you feel, that heaviness you carry on behalf of someone else, it could literally be the difference between their life and death. A number 8's emotional shoulders are broad, because God has given us the ability to carry a greater amount of weight. So if you are a number 8, you must consider what you stand for and why you stand for it. And when you stand for something or someone, don't apologize for it. Don't give up your voice.

My convictions become even more intense when it comes to my family. There are only three nonnegotiables: my wife, my daughter, and my son. I love my mother and my in-laws. I love my whole extended family. But I have to give an account for my wife and my kids. If I can't look them in the face because I have dishonored my personal convictions, then I'm not worth the skin I'm in. God didn't create me to be a yes man for someone else's agenda.

David wasn't agenda driven; he was kingdom driven. That's what happens when you're isolated and all you have is God. You want to please God. You don't care about pleasing people. And that's a kind of power for a number 8. Your mind is always on the deeper thing. Because of that, no one can talk you down from your position. You aren't stubborn. You aren't inflexible. But you are principled. When you have guiding principles and foundational stakes in the ground that you stand for, that's a life worth living. No, I will not allow you to do drugs around me. No, you aren't going to be around me and challenge other people's faiths. I don't have to believe what they believe, but we're not going to disrespect their faith tradition because our presence may be the only seed that introduces someone to Jesus.

Worshipping Warriors to the Rescue

When we look at the life of David, we often think about this mild, meek shepherd. We see him keeping helpless little lambs out of harm's way and singing sweetly into the sky. The Bible even calls him the Sweet Psalmist of Israel. But David goes from the shepherd's field to the battlefield within a very short time. He was still a teenager. He was still a singer. But he was also a warrior.

Robyn Carr at FamilyShare.com says,

> Although David was not skilled in the art of war, he had fought battles to protect his sheep. He had killed lions and bears when they attacked his sheep. He knew it was the Lord that had helped him defeat these enemies. With each success at protecting his flock, David was prepared for successive battles including his eventual face-off with Goliath. Each success gave him more confidence in his abilities. He didn't just show up at the battlefield having never relied on the Lord for strength.

The interesting thing is, that first time with Goliath, David wasn't looking for an opportunity to fight. He was going because he was asked to go by his father. I find it funny that, although he'd been anointed as the next king already, David was still treated like a regular dude in his house. If I'm honest, that would have probably made me real mad. I'm the next king and my brothers are still pushing me around and pranking me.

No, I don't think so.

I often imagine that David, like any little brother, fantasized busting his brothers over the head. Maybe that's just what I would have done. Don't judge me.

But David was a number 8, so he internalized it all. It's possible that two very distinct sides of himself were born from the internalization of pain. There was the sensitive man who worshipped God and wrote songs that blessed the Lord, and growing simultaneously alongside that part of himself was the raging man. And, of course, there's this perfect moment where David is given the opportunity to take the rage produced by the pain of his process, along with his righteous indignation, out on somebody who absolutely deserves it: Goliath.

Where did this little boy get the boldness to say to this man of war that he would fight him even when the armies of the Living God were afraid to do so? Nobody wanted a piece of Goliath, and it took a kid to be a man because he was surrounded by men who were boys. Where did this strength come from?

Glad you asked.

It came from being laughed at and isolated and rejected. It came from the powder keg of rage that had been building. It didn't take much to set David off, especially when the protection of others or the name of God was at stake.

Yes, he was super sensitive, but he also grew up to be someone who killed for a living. In fact, there was so much blood on his hands, the Bible says he wanted to build a temple for God and then God said, "Nah, D. You got too much blood on your hands. I'm going to let your son build me a house" (see 1 Chron. 28:3).

As number 8s like David, I think we really need to sit with this dynamic in order to understand ourselves better. The sweet psalmist of Israel had many, many bodies on his proverbial belt. He was a sensitive killer. One day he is like "I love you, God. Bless the Lord, oh my soul, and all that is within me, bless His holy name" (see Ps. 103). The next day he's slaughtering Philistines by the hundreds. I imagine him leaving the battlefield with not just blood on his hands but also on his face.

A contradiction? Maybe.

Number 8s are both worshippers and warriors. There's a part of us that's ready to war. We are on heightened alert, ready to battle. We struggle with trusting people. We trust God. We are skeptical of everyone else. This is because we see people. Not with our eyes, either. We have elevated levels of discernment in our souls, and we can spot fake people a mile away. I am a master of identifying inauthentic people. That was part of my field training. There was a part of me that learned how to mask my own pain and hurt, but in turn, I could recognize quite easily the masks that other people were wearing. I was able to spot when other people were hiding things.

This is what I call an unfortunate gift because number 8s don't always want to see what we see. We're empathic, remember? We're protectors, remember? So there is a strong likelihood that if we see the pain, we'll end up carrying it. But a true number 8 doesn't use someone else's pain to their advantage. We extend grace a thousandfold to the mask wearers we come across.

Why?

Because we know that every number 8 has his or her kryptonite. So we too are in desperate need of grace and mercy. We love God. We serve God. But there's always that area of weakness that keeps us running back to Him. And sometimes, the issues that are chronic and continuous in our lives are not going to go away for that very reason. Because they keep us running back to God. Because God cannot allow the raging warrior part of us to go unchecked. We must be willing to submit to the Lord for instruction and discipline.

David had residual value as a warrior because he was a worshipper too. He was submitted to God. A man or woman with that kind of rage that's not submitted to God can cause tremendous damage to people who don't deserve it. Even to the very people they have been called to stand up for and defend.

Number 8s have to be very careful about being emotionless. I've learned that we can have great amounts of empathy for people and simultaneously feel nothing. And when we are finished with the person, we have a tendency to cut them off for good and feel nothing. It's really scary to be at a place where you have deep abiding emotions, but when you are hurt or offended in the wrong moment, by the wrong person, it's like they never existed. That's another reason why we need to keep running back to God. Because the warrior in us is ready to "kill" anything that will bring us pain. And the way we run back to Him is through our worship. I'll discuss a little later the value of being a wounded worshipper.

Here's what you should know now though: God never wastes pain. Pain always has a purpose in the life of a number 8. But God will give you perspective about your pain. He will give you the ability to discern that your enemy is the one who deserves your wrath—not your brother or sister. Rest assured though, the pain of being overlooked and rejected will be used by God to build His kingdom.

I suppose this is the bottom line: Number 8s have a high sense of purpose. When that passion is stirred, it's almost impossible to make an 8 come down from their position. Number 8s fight from a heightened sense of moral obligation and are relentless when it comes to standing up for what they believe is right.

Number 8s are also warriors waiting in the wings for the right moment for them to arrive on the scene and fight. We don't choose the battles; they come to us. We don't look for the fight, but if the fight comes, we are ready. The power of an 8 is that we are peaceful worshippers by nature, but if provoked, an entirely different personality arrives on the scene from deep within our subconscious. That warrior, forged in the valley of loneliness, steeled by the pain of rejection, sharpened by the need to defend herself and those she is protecting against bigger, faster, stronger opposition, emerges from the shadows and breaks the back of an enemy that is caught unaware of what we carry in us.

Questions for Reflection

1. Specifically recount a moment when you felt righteous indignation stir in you.
2. When were you challenged to operate "above your pay grade," so to speak, in order to take on a Goliath-like foe?
3. In what ways have you personally put yourself in harm's way for another? Or maybe you observed someone making that sacrifice and it impacted you? Share the story.
4. What are some of the considerations you must make when choosing to fight for someone who can't fight for themselves? What are the risks? Rewards?

CHAPTER SEVEN

Big Me / Little King

It was time to go. God had made that clear to me. I'd been serving faithfully as a youth pastor at a wonderful church. I considered the pastor a father figure to me. But I had a rude awakening when I sat down with him to share that I felt like God was calling me into something new. This something new required traveling and was a way to do ministry in a different, creative way, a way that existed outside of the four walls of the traditional church.

He was not happy.

This leader, who I respected and admired very much, said to me: "I don't believe that this thing you are trying to do is the voice of the Lord, and you know if I pray about it, this whole thing will fall apart."

That hurt so bad. I'd served in that ministry devotedly.

I'd honored him every chance I could. I desperately wanted to be looked upon as a son by him. So to hear someone you love say that they could pray against you and your dreams will fall apart, well, I was devastated.

But I know what I'd heard. I responded by telling him that I had to respectfully maintain my position. It was time for me to move forward but I wanted nothing but the best for him and the church. I didn't say "who do you think you are?" We had a difference of opinion, but that wasn't going to make me dishonor him.

People in positions of authority are often caught off guard sometimes when they are faced with a number 8. I've seen leaders become insecure. Writer Shelly Webb says this in an Internet article:

> Any time an individual becomes exalted in a position, a job or any place of power, he or she immediately gains a new set of risks. With power comes feelings of pride and an air of confidence that can sometimes be the root of sin or other issues that may lead to sin. [We] should stay on guard against these types of dangers and learn from examples like David as to how to avoid those pitfalls.

Yes, we should. But most of the time leaders are secure because they don't particularly care for people they cannot control. In fact, when leaders can't control the narrative they often want to change the story. Over and over again, I've come across leaders who struggled with the Big Me/Little King syndrome. There were a few notable exceptions—men who understood what I carried and celebrated it. But they were just that, exceptions. When I say "Big Me," please know that I'm not making myself big in any self-aggrandizing way. I don't mean big in my own eyes. It just means that too many times when God decides to magnify what he has placed in us, people in positions of authority assume that we are their competition as opposed to an extension of their legacy.

The Oil Will Find You and That's OK

David wasn't looking for Saul's validation as much as he desired his love and mentorship. He didn't know what being anointed meant really. There was no frame of reference for him. And there was no way for him to change his situation or status in this society. He wasn't looking for anything, but I can assure you, the oil was looking for him. The significant thing about the anointing of David as king is that there were seven who went before him. And for those seven, the oil didn't flow. The oil didn't flow until he arrived. Why is this significant? Because you should know that as a number 8, you are not in competition with anyone else. Maybe if Saul understood that, he would have saved himself some trouble. It may be a church cliché, but that doesn't make it untrue. What God has for you, is for you. You don't have to worry about whether someone is going to come and take your position. If that position is yours, it's yours. Until it isn't anymore. Then it's there. You don't have any influence on that process. If you trust the Lord's planning and timing, He will get to you what belongs to you. You will have exactly what you're supposed to have.

The anointing we carry as number 8s, the significant specific enablement of God for our calling, is so unique that we are not in competition with anyone else. I've always been able to celebrate other people. I've never been jealous of anyone else's gift. Can I encourage you not to be jealous or insecure because someone else has a different gift, or what you would perceive as a more significant gift than yours? There are a diversity of gifts to build up the body of Christ. But there is no gift that is greater than another. They all complement one another. So we are not in competition with anyone; we are in concert with everyone. So let's learn how to celebrate our brothers and sisters who are walking this path of life and fighting for those who can't fight for themselves.

Some people will do anything for a position. I'm not one of them. David wasn't one of them. In fact, David was just the last kid on the totem pole, forgotten about. He's the one that got the oil. And let me encourage you in this. He had seven brothers in front of him. The prophet was trying to pour the oil on all seven of them. But God said no until He showed up. And then the oil was allowed to flow. Please take heart. You don't have to jockey for a position. You don't have to fight for approval. You don't need someone else's celebration of you. You don't need someone else to fail for you to succeed. The anointing that has your name on it, the calling, the gift that has your name on it, is irreversible and irrevocable. Your job is to be faithful, and everything with your name on it will get to you.

Yes, David wasn't looking for the oil, but the oil was looking for him. Attempting to usurp authority or to use our words to harm someone else is actually beneath a number 8. We don't have to do that. Our very lives prove the miraculous nature of the development of God.

André van Belkum on LifeHopeandTruth.com said this:

> Because of his wholehearted worship of God, David was richly blessed and became the greatest king to rule Israel. As a result of his righteous and effective leadership, the people of Israel experienced a time of national blessings and prosperity. It is clear that David was no usurper, but that it was God who placed him on the throne, a fact eventually recognized by the entire nation.

You can have all the gifts in the world, but if God doesn't choose you, it doesn't matter. Likewise, if you don't have any of the skills that you think you should have, if God has ordained you for a thing, he will elevate you. I am a living witness. I am not credentialed. I don't have advanced degrees in theology. But I firmly believe that I am anointed to preach the gospel. God is using me to build bridges among cultures and denominations not because I am so learned but because I have submitted to the work He has given me. You can't add anything to the anointing. You can only allow the anointing to seep into you and season you. You can let it settle you. You can be gifted and grow in your knowledge, but the anointing is the supernatural enabling power of God to manifest His purpose in the earth.

The anointing is reserved for those who will serve people like they literally have no time left. And as intense and as powerful as your calling is, and your gift is, the power of your calling, the power of your anointing, will not be in some grand display for all the world to see. The power of your anointing will be how you act once the moment of the platform is over. What did David do after he got anointed? Did he walk around with a velvet robe? Did he tilt his crown to the side and point at his brothers, screaming, "In your face suckers"? No. I believe that his character had been developed even at a young age to the point that once the anointing was done—while the oil was still fresh on his hair—he looked around and asked his dad, "Can I go back outside now?" With a shocked look, I believe Jesse whispered, "Yeah, son. Sure."

Knowing all this, no matter how "big" God says your anointing is, honor those little kings in your life.

It's About Honor

One of the things a number 8 can do to guard against some of these challenges with a leader and against an attack from the Sauls in our own lives is to go in honoring that person. Honor is the currency of elevation. I believe that every leader I've served will say I honored them, their wives, their children, and their vision. I've never served at a church where I wanted to be anything other than what I was asked to be. I've never entertained the conversations I'd hear from many people who would say, "You're so gifted, why don't you start your own church?" I quickly shut that down because that's the spirit of Absalom. Number 8s, though called themselves, do not usurp authority or try to take something that God never intended for them.

So many people want to be the "woman" or the "man." But sometimes just being one in the crowd that helps the vision is exactly where God wants you. So whether you are in ministry like me, in a professional or corporate setting, or in academia, your job is not to try to knock someone else out of position, but to maximize *your* position as best you can. If you make up in your mind and in your heart that you're going to honor no matter what, then you truly have the heart of a number 8.

And be clear. It's not about whether the other person honors you first or even if they ever honor you at all. Honor is about understanding God's authority and how God sets it up.

> Let every soul be subject to the governing authorities. For there is no authority except from God, and the authorities that exist are appointed by God. Therefore whoever resists the authority resists the ordinance of God, and those who resist will bring judgment on themselves. For rulers are not a terror to good works, but to evil. Do you want to be unafraid of the authority? Do what is good, and you will have praise from the same. For he is God's minister to you for good. But if you do evil, be afraid; for he does not bear the sword in vain; for he is God's minister, an avenger to *execute* wrath on him who practices evil. Therefore *you* must be subject, not only because of wrath but also for conscience' sake (Romans 13:1–5).

So if you have a leader, then honor him or her. That leader was placed there for a reason. You can learn something even in bad circumstances. Many times, when I kept seeing the same pattern, I learned what not to do as a leader.

I must say that there is definitely a difference between honoring a leader and accepting abuse. I'm not saying that you should let someone treat you like a rug they wipe their feet on. It's OK to stand your ground, in this regard, but you should still make the determination to honor that person.

The other part of honor, particularly when a situation is bad, such as when you are faced with the Big Me/Little King syndrome, is not allowing offense to overtake you. When you begin to ascend and start doing the things that your leaders may not want you to do, it is entirely possible that they may say or do things that hurt you. If you walk in a place of offense, then that offense can turn into unforgiveness. And unforgiveness can short-circuit everything the Lord wants to do in your life. John Bevere in his best-selling book *The Bait of Satan* digs into the impact that offense can have on believers and how we might turn away from it:

> When those who have been placed in my life to lead me and train me betray me and turn against me, as Saul turned against David, I will follow the example of David and refuse to let hope die in my heart. Holy Spirit, empower me to be a spiritual father or mother to those who need me to disciple, love, support, and encourage them. Father, raise up spiritual leaders in our land who can lead others with justice, mercy, integrity, and love. Allow me to be one of these leaders. When I am cut off from my father (physical or spiritual) through his insecurity, jealousy, or pride, cause me to recognize that as You did with David, You want to complete Your work in my life.

Holy Spirit, release me from tormenting thoughts or self-blame and striving for acceptance. Cause me to seek only Your acceptance and restoration. I refuse to allow the enemy to cause me to seek revenge against those who have wronged me. I will not raise my hand against the Lord's anointed or seek to avenge myself. I will leave justice to You. Father, cause my heart to be pure as David's was pure. Through Your power, O Lord, I will refuse to attack my enemies with my tongue, for I will never forget that both death and life are in the power of the tongue (Prov. 18:21). I will never seek to sow discord or separation between myself and my Christian brothers and sisters, for it is an abomination to my Lord. I will remain loyal to my spiritual leaders even when they have rejected me or wronged me. I choose to be a man [or woman] after the heart of God, not one who seeks to avenge myself. Holy Spirit, like David I will lead my Christian brother and sister to honor our spiritual leaders even in the face of betrayal. I refuse to sow discord among brethren. I will show kindness to others who are in relationship with the ones who have wronged me. Like David I will find ways to honor them and will not allow offense to cause me to disrespect them. Father, only You are worthy to judge the intents and actions of myself or of those around me. I praise You for Your wisdom, and I submit to Your leading. Lord, I choose to remain loyal to those in a position of authority over me. I choose to focus on the calling You have placed on my life and to refuse to be diverted by the actions of others, even when they have treated me wrongly. Father, may You be able to examine my life and know and see that there is neither evil nor rebellion in my heart toward others (1 Sam. 24:11).

For me, through very real relational pain, I'm going to honor my leaders. Through inevitable misunderstandings, I'm going to honor them. Because one day, I will have people under me, and I hope that the honor I've sown, I will reap.

He Missed His Heart

As I've said, David wasn't looking to become king. God chose him. Saul was still king when David became the talk of a nation. Surely Saul was grateful for David and the death of Goliath. But the insecure place in Saul manifested, of all places, after a song. As the king and his army were returning from battle, the ladies of the city were singing.

Whatever Saul asked David to do, David did it successfully. So Saul made him a commander over the men of war, an appointment that was welcomed by the people and Saul's officers alike. When the victorious Israelite army was returning home after David had killed the Philistine, women from all the towns of Israel came out to meet King Saul. They sang and danced for joy with tambourines and cymbals. This was their song:

"Saul has killed his thousands, and David his ten thousands!"

This made Saul very angry. "What's this?" he said. "They credit David with ten thousands and me with only thousands. Next they'll be making him their king!" (1 Samuel 18: 5–9)

Well, yeah.

Obviously, Saul didn't like the song. In fact, he hated the song. And he came to hate the one the song honored. So much so that he tried to kill him.

Saul tried to kill David not because he thought David wanted what he had. He killed him because he knew he didn't have what David did. There are some people who have plenty of position, money, authority, and notoriety, but they just can't seem to reconcile why they want to be you as opposed to the other way around. I've never wanted to be anybody other than who God made me. Once I came into an awareness of what God had for my life, I didn't want to be anybody else. And I was content to play the position that I was created to occupy.

Oh if Saul could have only seen the same in the heart

of David. David wanted no part of a monarchy. He just wanted to be loved. He wanted his king to be proud of him.

David just wanted to be accepted. He couldn't help that he was great. But the small mind-set and limited vision of King Saul caused him to miss the beauty of having a relationship with the best "son" he could have ever wanted.

The Nature of Sonship

What was really interesting about the pastor I mentioned at the beginning of this chapter was that over the years, as God continued to elevate me, that individual—who is a great leader in the body of Christ—welcomed me back. He called me son. And that was true. He was still my spiritual father and I his spiritual son. All I could say is, "Look at God." We didn't agree and there was certainly pain. But when there is sonship, the relationship dynamics don't change just because fears and trouble enter in. This is why I said that we cannot allow offense to infect our hearts. There is always the possibility of reconciliation. The Bible says God has given us the ministry of reconciliation (see 2 Cor. 5). That's not only just spiritually, where we are the vessels God uses to reconcile lost souls to their Creator. But that's also about reconciling ourselves to one another as the body of Christ. Whether in the church or on the job, pretty much in every area of your life, you will see yourself on

the fast track to relevance and longevity if you have cultivated a culture of honor where reconciliation after conflict
is possible.

But I must add this important point. All too often,
number 8s find themselves overachieving to honor those
we revere and respect. Don't do that. Sometimes those who
are leaders over us will assume the motive is not the need
for acceptance but pure ambition. Also, we could find ourselves exchanging the word God has given us for the word
of a man or woman—and missing our purpose altogether.
When this pastor told me that I shouldn't go, I could have
easily submitted to that voice, because he was a father figure and I loved him, despite the fact that his voice was dia-
metrically opposed to the voice of God I heard. That would
not have pleased God at all.

Sometimes wanting to be accepted will cause you to
miss God's blessing. As a number 8, you are going to take
the path less traveled. You have got to be willing to say,
"Yes, Lord, I heard your voice and I'm going to trust you."
This is where your faith is groomed. You will be developed
in a whole different way. That desire to be accepted and celebrated could have derailed me from my destiny. I would've
been stuck in a very nice church with really good people,
serving an excellent vision, but that would not have been
the sum total of what I was called to fulfill.

So the relational implications of this idea of sonship (and
daughters too!), particularly in the church, are important.

I've seen a lot of spiritual fathers and spiritual sons, and unfortunately, I've also seen some of those relationship dynamics manipulated. Particularly when it comes to men and women like me who don't have access to our earthly fathers. Spiritual leaders have a real responsibility to operate with honor, integrity, and character when stewarding individuals and navigating this area of sonship so that people are not injured further because they believed in a man. I've actually heard people say, "If you're my spiritual son, then you need to give me *x* number of dollars." I don't believe that's what sonship is. At all. I'm not asking the people I mentor and spend time with for a nickel. Especially when what God gave me, he gave me for free. If someone wants to so give a blessing to me and my wife, then that's fine. But I don't ask people for anything. I believe that if you're a leader, God takes care of you. You don't have to manipulate people's emotions to get that provision. I don't believe that the blessing of God is coming to a person because they gave a certain amount of money to an individual. Don't get me wrong! I am a tither. I believe in the principle of sowing into people. But I'm talking about leaders who manipulate relationships for personal gain.

Here's the thing. No child gets to choose their parents. A child arrives here through us and they get what they get. They are our progeny, whether they like it or not. But when it comes to sonship, nobody is forcing you to be or have a spiritual parent. Even when Jesus said, "Very truly

I tell you, unless you eat the flesh of the Son of Man and drink his blood, you have no life in you" (John 6:53) many people departed that very day. Jesus turned to his twelve disciples and said, "Will you bounce too?" (My interpretation, of course.) They said, "Where are we going to go? You have the words of life." But I don't think Jesus would have been mad if they did. He just wanted to know. He certainly didn't say, "Yo, if you leave, you won't be blessed."

The truth is, many of the most value-adding relationships in our lives are voluntary. I don't love my wife because I have to love her; I love her because I choose to love her. I volunteer my love daily to my wife. Every spiritual relationship should be voluntary in nature. If you are at a church where you feel like you are not being fed, take your family where you will be. Now if you have been offended and it is biblical truth making you want to leave, then search your heart to make sure it's not just you being unwilling to face the reality of changing your life. Know the differences between offense, bad teaching, and spiritual manipulation. Sonship is rooted in a voluntary relationship with the father. I believe if you have honored your spiritual parents but things don't work out, you can leave the relationship with your hands clean. You cannot serve a vision, if you don't have the heart of the leader. You cannot serve a ministry, if you don't honor the heart of your leaders. If you find yourself struggling to connect to the heart of the leader, then it might be time for you to make a different decision.

Questions for Reflection

1. Share a moment in your life when you found yourself fighting for the love and respect of the very people God was calling you to either replace or move into "their" arena. How did you manage that? What were the outcomes?

2. How do you think wanting to be accepted at all costs thwarts the plans of God for a number 8?

CHAPTER EIGHT

Dear Dad

My mother used to play games with me in our house. We'd play hide-and-seek in our tiny, two-bedroom apartment. We would make up tent cities with bedsheets and sticks, hanging them up so we could sit there and watch our little black-and-white TV. My mother always engaged me. She always made sure that my imagination was fostered and my creativity was expressed. But there were other aspects of my development that absolutely needed the touch of a dad. Even now, as a husband, a father, and knowing that my father died fifteen years ago, there are still times I glance out the window and wish my dad would come down the street like he promised.

After my mother and father divorced, my dad would occasionally call and speak with me. He would always call collect, normally from a bar. I could always tell he'd been drinking because his speech would be slurred. I didn't know what an alcoholic was at ten, eleven, and twelve years old. I didn't know that my father was battling with addiction. Despite what I'm sure was a deeply painful time for her, my mother never vilified my father in front of me. She never told me that he was a bad man who had a propensity for violence. She never told me how he had hurt her, let her down, and betrayed her trust. I didn't learn any of that until I was well into my adult years. I had no clue about my father's addictions to alcohol and drugs.

I just knew that dad was calling. He would say the strangest things.

"I worship the ground you walk on, and the air that you breathe." Or, the most comforting things.

"I love you my son."

He sounded so noble and stately, and in those few moments, because of those few inebriated words, I concocted an entire character of who my father was. I told people my dad worked in New York for some bigwigs in a crime family. (That was to keep the bullies off of me.) The truth though was less dramatic. Dad was an alcoholic jazz musician trying to make ends meet; he was living life the best he could, in spite of the regrets I'm sure he had. Nevertheless, I would live for his calls. And the desire to be fathered never left me even after the calls stopped.

I longed to be affirmed. To be accepted and celebrated. To be given direction and have someone believe in me. My mom did that, but I needed my dad to do it too. It's amazing to realize that your very life has been formed by your mother's presence and your father's absence. I needed my dad to be there. And at the most life-changing times, he wasn't.

When dad left, my mother was left to try to do the job of two individuals. But she couldn't be everywhere. One of those moments she couldn't be there, changed my life.

I was about four and a half years old. We lived at 806 East Mitchell Avenue. It was the middle of the day, and I was playing in the front yard. Two teenagers from the neighborhood approached me. One of them exposed himself to me. They both asked me to do something so despicable, so heinous. A sexual act. At four years old, I didn't know what to do. I didn't know what to say. I was so, so scared. So I did it.

I was sexually abused, in my front yard, in the middle of the day with cars driving by, and no one stopped. Even though the events that took place happened over a matter of seconds, they seemed like an eternity to me. They still do.

I was finally able to get up and away from those young men. My voice returned to me and I cried and yelled at them both. I told them, "I'm going to tell my mother!" One of them responded, "If you tell, *you'll* be the one who gets in trouble."

So I didn't tell.

And I didn't share this story with anybody until I was almost twenty years old.

My mother was in the house. The door was open. But she never saw it. She couldn't be everywhere. Moms, release yourself from the guilt you may feel because something awful happened to your child "on your watch." Take the *S* off your chest, you can't be everywhere.

As I walked up the steps of the porch and back into my house, my mother had no clue that my innocence had just been snatched. She had no idea that I had been introduced—illegally—to an area of life that is sacred, and beautiful, and holy. That area, sexuality, had just become dirty and perverted and dishonorable to me. And as a four-year-old, I had no capacity for grappling with what had just taken place.

One of the questions that would come up as I began to deal with what happened to me as a child was, "Where was my father?" A father would not allow that to happen to his child. My mother was doing the best she could. She didn't know that her baby had changed. That's how quick the enemy slipped in. That's how fast destiny can be altered. That's how fast legacy can be interrupted. But, in my mind, maybe, just maybe, it wouldn't have happened if my dad had been there.

To Be Truly Seen

I needed my dad. And for the longest time, I searched for one. I needed for somebody with authority to see me. Yet too many times in my development, there were people who I thought should have seen what I carried, but for whatever reason, they either chose not to help me develop it or they really did not see it. It wasn't until later that I understood that sometimes even the most keen eye can't see deep-seated greatness. Remember the prophet Samuel at Jesse's house looking to anoint a king? When he saw Eliab, the oldest son of Jesse, he said, "This has got to be the next king of Israel." And it was God who spoke to the prophet and said, "Do not anoint him, for I have refused him, for man looks at the outside, God looks at the heart" (see 1 Sam. 16:6–8). So sometimes even prophets can't see what you carry.

A study from Regency College's Marketplace Institute about David's anointing says:

> Outward appearances—background, physical attrac-tiveness, knowledge, skills, experience—important as they are, are not the most important qualifications. In our age of image-politics, where being telegenic and having excellent communication skills are con-sidered the most important prerequisites to political success, this is extremely hard advice to take seriously. It seems so counter-intuitive as to be almost foolish.
>
> Even Samuel, in assessing the suitability of the var-ious sons of Jesse for the kingship, almost repeated the same mistake he had made in assessing Saul's qualifi-cations, i.e., putting too much faith in an impressive physical appearance. When Eliab, Jesse's first-born

son and apparently an impressive figure, appeared
before Samuel, his immediate thought was, "Surely
the Lord's anointed stands here" (I Samuel 16:6).

But I sure tried to make myself seen, that's for sure. I
grew up in a small community of mostly women. And I've
already told you that I wasn't the cool kid. Well I was especially awkward when it came to interacting with women.
I didn't have the confidence to even engage in just casual
conversation. There I was, a young boy in his prepubescent
years trying to navigate hormones and the awakening and
awareness of his own masculinity juxtaposed against a very
strict religious background that didn't lend itself toward
grace. It was a cocktail for emotional disaster. My mother,
phenomenal woman of God that she is, was committed to
prayer and teaching the word. But she came from a very
different background. The Bible is black and white for her.
Don't do this, don't do that. The Bible was very clear, for
her, on behavior. However, what I didn't know then, and
do now, is that there's grace for the process. I've learned
that we must give people room to grow, space to breathe.

I needed my dad. I needed grace.

It All Goes Back to Dad

After my mom and dad divorced, and being too young to
understand the family dynamics, I sensed that there was

something lacking, something missing. Again, I can't emphasize enough how great my mother was by any measure or metric. But there's something to be said about the power of identity.

In the case of David, growing up in a Middle Eastern, patriarchal society, the father held tremendous power. Fathers had the authority to declare purpose, destiny, in fact, identity into their children. What is significant about David is that we find that his father is so unaware and disconnected from the greatness that he was raising, that he didn't even see the potential of his own son. When the prophet showed up and said, "There's a king in your house," he invites his first seven sons to stand up. Not the eighth.

When Samuel came looking for a king, the seven sons were anxiously awaiting the possibility of being the one. But David was outside doing what he had always done. He had been relegated to menial tasks. He was given the things that the other brothers thought were beneath them. He was in full view of his brothers and his father, but he was still not seen.

I wondered how David felt in that field. All he had were a few sheep, an open field, some songs, and his heart for God. He didn't know that the monotony of his day-to-day routine was developing in him a military genius, an artistic and creative virtuoso. This isolation by his father created a polarizing nature in David that he wrestled with his entire life. On the one hand he was known as a worshipper who wrote love songs to God. But he also became a king, a vicious warrior who could slay tens of thousands of people. It would not seem that those two dynamics would exist inside of one man, but he may have had to become both of those things in order to survive his surroundings, to survive what was missing in his family life.

I believe that everything in David's life, good and bad, can be traced to his relationship with his father. As mentioned earlier, in ancient Israel, it was the duty of the father to declare identity. David was anointed king of a nation in front of a father who never saw him. Therefore, everything in David's life centered around needing the validation, direction, and wisdom of a father.

The Legacy of the Fatherless

Despite fatherlessness, God still has a plan for our lives. God's purpose will prevail. David was in the middle of a field. All he heard was his father's voice calling him. As he walked, he had no clue that his entire life was about to change, that his whole world was about to shift because a collision was taking place between the father who raised him, from whom he longed for acceptance, and the heavenly Father, who would keep him.

The legacy of the fatherless, particularly for a number 8, is a constant longing, a constant aching, and a desire to be seen and validated by someone in a position of authority.

It's also a constant battling against an enemy who uses our fatherlessness to try to thwart our purpose.

I believe it was the plan of the enemy to snatch not only my innocence that day in my front yard, but also to confuse my identity in a failed hope that I would blame God for what happened. I hear all the time people saying, "Why does God allow bad things to happen? Why would God allow something like that to happen to a little child?" If I'm honest, I've asked that question a time or twenty myself. But the other side of that question is, What kind of God would create the opportunity for good and evil to exist? And the ultimate question: Did God create evil?

No, God created choice.

Man created evil, and this is how we exist in a spiritual and natural world. We must choose which path to take. Every decision leads us down a very real path to a very real conclusion. If you make honorable choices, holy choices, God honors them. And on the other side of that, if you make ungodly and dishonorable choices, you will reap the fruit of that as well. God didn't create evil. God created man. Man was given choice. I believe that anything that happens in the life of a believer is either God-ordained or God-allowed. God did not want that bad thing to happen to me, but somehow He made it so that it did not define me.

Another beauty that came from the ashes of my fatherlessness was that I was fortunate enough not to grow up resenting my father or the concept of fatherhood altogether.

My lack actually made me want to be a better father. It made me want to be the thing I never saw. And so what the enemy meant for bad, got turned around for good. I forgave my dad. I forgave those two teenagers who abused me.

How was I able eventually to get to a place where I was able to forgive those who hurt me? I learned to be able to discern the character of God, even when I couldn't see the face of God. Remember, I am a number 8. I gained power from being in the field. Yes, for a while there, I felt like I was out in the wilderness trying to figure things out, trying to navigate feelings and emotions that were foreign. But over time God showed me how he was using those broken places to form greatness in me. That greatness would not have been able to come through fully if I had held on to hostility toward the very things and people that God had used to form it in the first place.

And now, that generational curse is broken. I have created my own legacy.

My kids don't know a time when I wasn't there. I saw my father four times in my life. We went to see a movie together when I was no more than ten years old. We flew a kite in a thunderstorm. Another time, I remember my mother sliding money into his hand to take me to get something to eat because he didn't have it. And right before he died. But because I've created a new legacy for myself, this will never be my children's lot. For that, God gets all the glory.

Making My Dad(s) Proud

My desire for fathering, for nurturing, for a connection to someone bigger than myself, higher than myself, actually pushed me into a relationship with God. Even though my earthly father, for whatever reason, didn't want to spend time with me, I had a heavenly father who loved me. I had a Savior named Jesus who believed in me, and who gave His life for me. Even as a young child those concepts of sacrifice, covering, and protection, rang true in those hollow, empty places that existed from not having a father present.

The longing for a father kept me teachable. I was always waiting for someone to lead me. That serves me well now because no matter what I do in any area of my life, I'm always looking for whoever the leader is so that I can honor them.

But I didn't just want my dad around so that he could teach me things. I wanted my dad around so that I could love him. Even though I'd only spent a few moments face-to-face with my father, I knew that there was a consistent sadness to him, and I wanted to make him proud. I wanted to be something that brought joy to him. I wanted him to smile. And even now, whether it's with my pastor or leaders, or church and speaking engagements I take, I always try to honor the visionary or leader. I know this stems from my longings, from wanting to please. In many ways, it's great. In other ways, it can be debilitating. All of it is linked to wanting to have my father close.

My dad's name, that's what I carry. He was John W. Gray Jr. I'm John W. Gray III, and no matter how much I'd love to be able to run from some of the things he did and the man that he was, the reality is, I would not be here if it weren't for him. I exist as an extension of his name, but I can be the beginning of a restored legacy. There is nothing like the power of legacy. There's nothing like the power of starting over. There's nothing like the power of a new beginning. Don't forget, that's the power of number 8.

As number 8s, we long to be connected to the divine nature of God by virtue of His presence. We long for God's father essence. We somehow know that it is in the presence of God that we find clarity of purpose, surety of identity, and focus for the future. Whether with our earthly fathers or our heavenly Father, we search for our father's stamp of approval in almost anything we do. We want to make our dads proud.

Questions for Reflection

1. If you are fatherless, how have you been able to reconcile the pain of that with what God is doing in your present and your pursuit of purpose?

2. If you are not fatherless, did your father speak your identity into you? How have you benefited from having a father's guidance?

3. What are the relational implications on both sides when a "son" is not seen by a "father"?

CHAPTER NINE

Scavenger Hunt

I was in pain, internally and externally. I'd never been in an ambulance before. I'd never stayed in a hospital before. This was not how things were supposed to go.

It was all going to be so sweet. I was going to host the Forward '06 conference and preach in New Brunswick, New Jersey, at one of the greatest churches on earth. Then I was going to MegaFest. It was supposed to be the greatest two weeks of my life.

Be careful what you pray for. I'd prayed the Wednesday before in front of the whole church. I'd started calling out principalities and rulers of wickedness in high places and told them that if they wanted to attack my pastor and my church, they had to go through me.

Right.

So the next night, before Bishop Jakes gets out of his car (his dressing room was right up the hallway from mine), I stood onstage to prepare the crowd for warfare praise and a life-changing word. I began to sense the presence of God and then, as I do from time to time, began to jump straight up and down.

Then it happened.

Right when the crowd was shouting praises up to God with absolute passion and power, I jumped up and came down one last time when I heard something snap. It felt like I'd fallen through a hole in the stage. I hadn't. I'd blown out my knee.

I fell to the stage in front of seven thousand kids and did the unthinkable: I continued to lead worship. I told the kids to continue to bless the name of the Lord. I dropped the microphone for a brief second and motioned for the stage-hands to help me. They ran up onstage and lifted me up. I told the crowd that if they wanted to see a miracle, then here I was. I knew I'd messed up my knee pretty bad, but I had no idea just how bad. But I sang, broken knee and all, right there in front of everyone and told them that God was still good. I fought off tears until I got off the stage. Then, I cried and cried and cried. Yes, because of the pain, but something else too. How could this have happened to me now? Why would God do this to me this week of all weeks? What did I do wrong?

I'd totally ruptured my patellar tendon and dislocated my kneecap. It is the kind of pain that is described online in search results for this condition as "extraordinary." They were correct. Even when I was on heavy medication, the pain was intense.

I had to have surgery, and I'm not going to lie, this was a hard one to trust God on. He didn't just mess with my schedule, but He also messed with my money. I'd lost so much. I needed that dough to pay bills and stuff. It's not like I'd broken my knee trying to twerk at the club. I was ministering to His people. Have you ever tried to explain something to God after He's already made a decision? That's where I was. The doctor said I would be down for eight weeks. He also said I couldn't fly because of the risk that blood clots could kill me.

The Lord *is* my shepherd; I shall not want. He makes me to lie down in green pastures; He leads me beside the still waters... (Psalm 23:1–2)

No kidding.

I admit I was angry. I thought this was my coming-out moment. All of these great opportunities were here because I had earned them, right? Wrong. God was showing me that my pride had gotten in the way of the truth: Yes, I'm a number 8. Yes, He has designated me for a purpose, but I don't deserve my platform.

It's only by grace I was and am able to stand.

I had forgotten that. I thought that I had arrived. I hadn't. Speaking the word of God is a privilege, not a right. I thought

I was somebody special. I was so special I had stopped praying before preparing for sermons, relying on my own ability. I was so anointed that I stopped reading my word altogether. I was totally content to operate in my own ability. That's what I was serving and that's what people were eating. And they kept eating. I was supposed to be bringing a life-changing word to people who desperately needed the presence of the King of Glory, not another personality. People don't need more people. They need people who get out of the way and show people the one true God! I had forgotten that too.

I wasn't broken enough. God needed me to see the true condition of my heart. *Stop trying to walk around like you've arrived, John. Stop walking around like you're the man. Stop walking altogether.* As a matter of fact, maybe God allowed my knee to buckle because I was too stubborn to get on my knees on my own. I'd heard God calling me closer for some time. But for some strange reason, I was afraid of Him. But busting my knee forced me into His presence, and I'm so glad. It was where I needed to be all long.

In my pain, God sent me on a kind of scavenger hunt that, if I could find all the authentic pieces of myself, would return me back to Him.

Running into Yourself

Now Saul spoke to Jonathan his son and to all his servants, that they should kill David; but Jonathan,

Saul's son, delighted greatly in David. So Jonathan told David, saying, "My father Saul seeks to kill you. Therefore please be on your guard until morning, and stay in a secret *place* and hide" (1 Samuel 19:1–2).

Saul couldn't take it anymore. David had to die. So he tried to kill him. Twice. Either he was super dense and couldn't take a hint, or David was so in need of affirmation and fathering that he took the near-death experience as a necessary evil. As we've uncovered, it was probably a little bit of both. I wonder if, in David's mind, anything was better than going back to the field of the forgotten. Better to die remembered, than to live forgotten.

But after a certain point, David had to go. Off he went, into the woods, the fields, the caves, running, barely sleeping, and eating whatever he could. All because he was too great to be small. Saul thought he drove David away, but he actually accelerated his ascension. Running for his life, David actually ran into his life. He picked up pieces of himself all along the way. What began as a manhunt for Saul, also became a scavenger hunt for David, where he picked up clues on how to lead, love, and serve in the worst of times.

Clues for Destiny

The Bible says that God can declare the end from the beginning. This means God writes backward but we live it forward. So God allows us to start our lives with the end in mind. In developing you, He starts with where He wants you to end up. Then every day He monitors your choices to see how you will end up there.

This is not puppetry. God is not in heaven pulling strings. We are not Pinocchio. We are autonomous beings who have the spirit of God, but all of us are unique in that we do have free will. But for those of us who have submitted to the lordship of Christ, we have unlocked another level of intimacy and relevance.

Relevance is one of the key components of the enduring legacy of a number 8. We are not relevant to just a particular time, because the anointing has no expiration date. Our anointing is not a fragrance that has been manufactured and will eventually wear off of us. We have the ability to have the fragrance of our anointing outlast our lifetime and extend as an echo into eternity.

I believe David, after being anointed by God, went back out in that field and watched the sheep because that's the kind of leader God is looking for. He's looking for those who will not be impressed with their own oil because, after all, they didn't produce it and they did not call themselves. They were called by God, and when you know you were called by one greater than yourself, you don't walk in pride. You walk in humility, knowing that you've been chosen, not because of who you are, but in spite of who you are. Some people might say, "What's the big deal? It was just oil. It's just oil." Yeah, it's just multiple compounds that create a fragrance and an aroma, and the oil by itself has limited value. But it was who was behind the oil that has all the value. It adds the value to the oil. God determined David was the one, not just to get the oil or the anointing, or in the Hebrew, the smearing. (It literally means "God touches you.") But God also determined that the oil would be smeared on the forehead, like a swiping of the forehead saying "I've put my hand on you." And you cannot overstate the power of God putting his hand on the flesh.

The anointing oil, according to the Old Testament, was never supposed to touch the flesh of a man. It was supposed to touch only the garments that the priests would wear. But in this Scripture, the oil touched the flesh of David. This is significant for us as number 8s because this was the first time that the oil touched the broken nature of humanity. I believe it was God saying, "I am going to work and work alongside humanity knowing its limitations. I'm still going to allow my oil to flow." Please don't disqualify yourself from being a leader. Please don't disqualify yourself from being used by God because of the issues of life or bad decisions that you've made. Be encouraged that God would pour his oil on broken humanity. This is the beauty of God's plan for those of us who have been broken, those of us who wish we could make different decisions, those of us who know we've blown it and don't deserve the goodness of God. But of our own effort and will, God says, "That's the heart I can use and that is a heart I can multiply. That is a heart I can trust."

Neither my past mistakes nor my present struggles are any match for the anointing. What the anointing declares is that God has made up His mind. It's like going to a car lot and picking out the car that you want, the interior color, the external paint, all of the trim, the wheels, the engine, and your preferences might not be what someone else would choose, but it speaks to your heart. Do you know that you are a one-of-a-kind masterwork, a masterpiece of God's creative ingenuity? When He looks at you, He sees exactly what He wants to get glory out of, and you'll say, "But I got a lot of miles on my car." Well, take heart. God knows how to reconstruct the engine. He knows how to retread the tires. God knows how to reframe and refit your life so that even from the ashes of the worst decisions and moments, He can produce a sweet oil, a gift of a life from the pain of a broken past. God can turn it around.

That's the power of the anointing. I may not be the most gifted person but I'm anointed. I may not be the best preacher but I'm anointed. I may not be the best singer but I'm anointed to worship. I'm anointed to declare God's word. I know that. I have no doubt about it, and whatever deficiencies I have, the anointing makes the difference. The anointing makes up the difference. The scope and influence of your anointing is directly proportional to the posture of your heart. So many people have gifts and talents that God would love to use, but their hearts have been corrupted and they're unwilling to be corrected. If you are corrupted and unwilling to be corrected, then you are convinced that you, relying on just your own power, have the ability to change people's lives. And in certain areas of life, that could be true, but when it comes to the spiritual nature of the Divine calling, it's on your life, and you need the enabling power of God.

So how do number 8s find the clues we need about ourselves, the spiritual bread crumbs, that will lead us to our destiny, especially when, like David, we are feeling broken and chased. Well first, the Bible says, "the steps of a righteous man are ordered by God" (see Ps. 37:23).

It's almost like God takes a step back and says, "I wonder what they're going to do here." As if there are some things that He chooses not to know. I know that that sounds crazy and maybe a bit heretical, because the Bible says God is omniscient—He knows all things. Dr. Robert Morris once said that "God doesn't just know all things, he knows all things at the same time." In other words, nothing has ever occurred to God. He's never said, "I never thought of that before." Because He has.

And in the big scheme of things, there are many who would say, "Well, if God knows everything, how can I ever make a choice on my own?"

God has given us free will. He doesn't manipulate outcomes, but He is committed to them. He loves us so much, in that way. He has an "expected end" for us.

For I know the thoughts that I think toward you, saith the Lord, thoughts of peace, and not of evil, to give you an expected end" (Jeremiah 29:11).

I believe that God has an expected end for his children. Well what about sickness and accidents, you ask? What about people who die too soon? Now we are getting into the sovereignty of God—something that is truly above my pay grade. There are certain things I don't know and that none of us will ever know while here on earth. I don't know why my best friend died at twenty-four. I don't know why some of my friends died of gunshot wounds and I'm still alive. I don't know why my cousin Rex died of AIDS. I don't know why any of it had to happen. There are choices we make, and sometimes those choices have consequences. Other times, it has nothing to do with us but has something to do with someone else making a bad choice, and we are affected by it. This is where my faith becomes the only thing that I can hold on to. I have to believe that "And we know that all things work together for good to them that love God, to them who are the called according to his purpose" (Rom. 8:28).

So there's a part of me that doesn't understand all the things that happen in the world and all the things that happened to me. But I trust God. I've made my decision about God.

I will never accuse Him. That doesn't mean I agree with everything or understand everything He does, but I made my decision.

Another important thing for a number 8 to do is start walking. David said, "Yea, though I walk through the valley of the shadow of death, I will fear no evil: for thou art with me; thy rod and thy staff they comfort me" (Ps. 23:4). What I love about this is, it wasn't the substance of death. It wasn't a form of death. It was a shadow. And wherever there is shadow, there is a light.

I preached that sermon some years ago and I've heard it in varying forms from other communicators, but I love this idea that David was walking. It's the most significant part of that passage. Nope, not the valley. Not even the shadow. I'm walking through all of it. I'm moving forward. I wrote a song called "Journey" and it talks about *red lights and green lights and stop signs and highways and toll booth and potholes and people who don't want you to make it, and sometimes you can't take it, but you can't let nothing rock you, please don't let the devil stop you on your journey.*

Don't stop, 8. Keep walking.

But what if I'm walking the wrong way?

The steps of a righteous man are ordered by the Lord, remember? That word *righteous* doesn't mean righteous in your own power or that you're perfect. Of course you're not perfect! We are only made right because of the finished work of Jesus Christ. But this *righteous* literally means that your heart is determined to honor God. So even if you're walking the wrong way, you can trust that God will lovingly steer you in the right direction.

Sometimes you won't see the clues to your destiny until you're already where you're supposed to be. There are certain things that took place in my life that might have looked liked serendipity or happenstance but they were absolute

markers for my journey. I remember when I was with Kirk
Franklin and The Family at one of our concerts and the
group DC Talk was there. DC Talk is a well-known Contemporary Christian group. Their manager was named
Dan, and he was a phenomenal man, a real bridge builder.
He was committed to the work of racial reconciliation
within the body of Christ. I remember them coming to talk
to Kirk and I just "happened" to go to his dressing room
while they were there. They were discussing the potential
of a tour promoting equality and eliminating racism in the
church. Now this was 1996 to 1997, so it was a really novel
idea, particularly in the music industry, where the line of
gospel music versus Christian music was still very stark.
Contemporary Christian was code for "white people singing." Gospel was code for "black people singing."

I never understood that. Jesus isn't white or black. He
is not American. Jesus was a Middle Eastern Jew born in
Bethlehem, raised in Nazareth, who walked around Israel
in the Middle Eastern heat. So whatever Jews looked like
then, in those conditions, that's what he looked like. And
most importantly, it wasn't his color that made the difference; it was the blood. People, especially in America, have
utilized a racialized Jesus to form their own theologies and,
at times, to marginalize other people. But that's not what
Dan was trying to do. I got a chance to talk to him later
and shared with him how much I loved the idea, and if
they needed a host, I would love to be considered. They

offered me an opportunity to tour with them and I met some wonderful people. We toured all over the country trying to build bridges and make the body of Christ more reflective of the beauty of heaven.

Looking back, that experience was a critical "clue" for me, an important critical place of development in 1997 that has served me well in 2013 when I took my current position at the largest church in this country, which also happens to have the most diverse congregation in this country. Because of that tour, I learned different ways of communicating with people from different backgrounds about the truth of Jesus. I was able to do it in a way where I didn't lose the attention of my core audience. That experience served as spiritual bread crumbs that led me to pieces of myself I did not know existed but are integral parts of me today.

Your life as a number 8 will feel a lot like puzzle pieces. I just want to encourage you and say follow behind the Lord and keep walking. If you don't feel His presence, if you don't feel peace, then that's a clue. If you are feeling unrest in an area, get moving. The one thing that could ruin everything is you standing still. So many people say, "I'm not moving until God tells me to." Well, in many cases, God has already told you to move, he just hasn't told you where. Don't believe me? Ask Abraham. God said to Abraham, leave your father and mother's house and go to a land I will show you. We want God to tell us where we are going and how to get there. He doesn't always do that. Trust that

He will show you where to walk. It doesn't count as faith if He tells you. That's just obedience, and that's easy

Keep in mind God desires glory. He is concerned about developing every area of your life. Once we are fully mature, we produce glory for His Kingdom, and when God speaks know that He will never contradict His Word so make sure that the voice you hear lines up with the Word you read. The principles of His word, will give the strength you need to trust His heart even when you can't see His face.

I'm training my children to honor what I say even if they don't see me in their face. It's the same way with God. He's not trying to keep you on one of those parent leashes I see in the malls these days. He wants you to be fully mature and well equipped to do the work of the ministry until the end of time. Yes, sometimes He will train you by His silence. But the silence of God is not always His displeasure. Many times it is His development. God is training you to walk when you don't hear His voice because you already got a word from Him and you trust His character.

You will also find nuggets for your journey in your daily devotional time and your daily prayer life. You'll find them as you stay in fellowship with like-minded individuals. Bad company corrupts good character. If you really want to get to destiny, find other people who are trying to get there too. So study your word, stay in prayer, and continue positive fellowship are three critical action steps for number 8s. I personally have surrounded myself with people who I know love God, and even to this day, I stay connected to men who love God and who are trying to do the things I'm trying to do: be a good husband, a good father, and a faithful son. If I can do those three things, I will have lived well and died right.

Where My Heart Lies

When I hurt my knee, I felt like God had stopped my ascent. But He also stopped my descent. He cared enough to correct and adjust my character and motives and attitude so that I could be a man of God, humble and broken enough to be trusted with the souls of believers worldwide. I needed that moment. I couldn't go to the next level, another field trip, if you will, because God hadn't signed the permission slip. So MegaFest was going to go on without me. My other obligations had to wait until I was sufficiently healed, physically and otherwise. Until I was made perfectly whole, I needed to sit still.

For many number 8s, the love we lost, the mistakes we made, the people who rejected us, actually propel us to who we were always called to be. As we are running toward destiny, we find bits and pieces of ourselves along the way. We find clues to destiny in the most broken of places. The journey of the dispossessed becomes the pathway for coronation.

Questions for Reflection

1. Have you ever found yourself running for your life? Maybe not literally but spiritually or psychologically? Share a story from that experience about how that running did or did not lead you to the pieces of yourself you needed to fulfill purpose.

2. How will you find the clues you need, the spiritual bread crumbs, that will lead you to your destiny— especially on those days when you are feeling broken and chased?

CHAPTER TEN

Hearts and Parts

When I was growing up, I didn't want to be a preacher. I wanted to be a deacon. Deacons in my black Baptist church were so cool. They got to sit in the front row. They got to sing songs at the beginning of service. They wore snazzy suits and drove Cadillacs. They gave out communion. And they even got to sleep while the pastor was preaching. They were the masters of acting like they weren't asleep. It was like they had an inner alarm that detected a pause in the sermon, when they would jump up and say, "Amen" or "Preach now." Then they'd go back to sleep.

I wanted to be a deacon so bad that I joined a program my church had called Junior Deacon. We literally got to shadow the deacons. On Saturday afternoons, we would help fill the communion trays with 100 percent premium

Welch's grape juice (Concorde grape, of course). We'd break up the salt-less kosher crackers while wearing our special white gloves. When the elders weren't looking I would sneak and eat a bunch, because one can't be a teenager around crackers and grape juice and not want to drink and eat it all.

I wanted to be a deacon because it seemed like they were the ones who touched the people. My pastor, Dr. Wayne Davis, was very learned and credentialed. He had earned a doctorate of theology. Part of that process, I think, made him not only so brainy and knowledgeable but also, at times, very disconnected from the "regular" people in the congregation.

As a kid, I would always try to connect with him. He was another father figure for me, but I could never crack that distance. I remember being in sixth grade; I took a test to go to the prestigious Walnut Hills School—the number one high school and middle school in Cincinnati. I took the test and I passed with the highest score in my school. My pastor graduated from Walnut Hills, and I remember him being so proud of me. So proud that he bought me this amazing Wembley tie. It was a yellow silk with a small blue paisley with little dots and a little red in it also. The feeling that came over me wearing that tie was indescribable. He was proud of me and I basked in that feeling.

Unfortunately after I started attending Walnut Hills, I didn't do so well. I never really studied, and with my mom's schedule she never made a huge deal out of checking my homework. She'd ask. I'd lie. That was it. So my grades were not good. At the beginning of eighth grade, I was still not doing well and the school decided that I needed a different, less rigorous curriculum.

I begged the principal to let me stay, but they had made up their mind. When I told my pastor I was leaving he was so disappointed. "Why would you leave?! The hardest days are behind you!" I didn't have the guts to tell him that I wasn't keeping up. I suspect the disappointment was deep for him too. There weren't a whole lot of young men in the church that were active. I was the most active boy there. But after that, I felt a kind of distance emerge between us. I still sought his approval, but the tension never really went away.

Oh but the deacons?! They nurtured me. Deacon Simon Jones, Deacon Thomas Danner, these men who had to be in their sixties then and grew up in the Jim Crow South took me under their wings. Deacon Danner was the leader of the Boy Scout troop and he would take us camping. We went fishing and to baseball games. I remember Deacon Jones bought me a blue jean, button-down shirt. It was beautiful. And I couldn't believe he'd bought it just for me.

Although we were a midwestern city above the Mason-Dixon line, these guys had southern sensibilities and strong traditions, and they instilled some of that in me. They spoke into me very early on and stabilized my yearning for a father soul.

But they weren't the only ones.

When I left Walnut Hills, I was nervous because it was a predominantly white school and I was headed to a predominately black school. I didn't know what to expect or how to behave, and there I was, immediately thrust into a whole other level of team culture. A culture I hadn't experienced before. It was a convergence for sure. There was this new thing called hip-hop, my conservative mother, and my gospel tendencies to contend with. Throw in some raging hormones and no real conversation about sex or dating and you have one mixed-up teenage boy heading to the high school. This was for sure a wilderness moment.

I battled through all of the same things that most young men battle through. But a saving grace for me was Justin Taylor, my best friend. We met the first day of our ninth grade year because we rode the same bus. Justin was a snazzy dresser. Instead of a book bag, he would carry a briefcase to school. Now there was nothing in the briefcase, but I still thought that was the most amazing thing to me. We became fast friends, and though we were the same age, he was like a big brother to me. Justin had been exposed to more. He was a ladies' man. Not the cutest guy in the world, but he knew how to talk to the ladies. I learned from him that you don't have to be cute. If you got good lyrics, you can get a girl.

So whether it was Justin, other friends, or one of the deacons from my church, I was able to find my tribe despite my encounters with bullying when I was younger. I remember that each one of my friends had a significant gift, but together we thought we were like the X-Men, unstoppable. We were this amazing team with lots of heart.

I think that's what David was able to do with the men that served him. He was able to tap into the pain and anguish of these men, who were like him in many ways. It wasn't about talent. It was about the heart. And that mirrors how God develops us. It's always about heart. There are tons of skilled people, but the heart is what is paramount to God. How do you treat people? Do you have sufficient humility? Do you honor them without having to get something in return?

That's what I learned during those years. With all the different things that come with being a teenager, I found myself connecting to different people for different things. I didn't have just one David. I had many different Davids in many different forms over the years. And I think that was God's intention. He wanted me to glean something from one person over here, connect to this gift over there, observe this character flaw here. God was stitching me together by fulfilling my longings and needs through connections with different people.

I didn't have a father to declare a prophetic destiny over me, and maybe neither have you. Therefore, there are parts of us that have been framed and developed by the relationships and interactions we've had over the years. Don't despise the fact that there is not just one individual that you can look to for guidance. God did that for a reason. You are a number 8 and God doesn't want anyone else to stand up and say, "I made you." No one is going to individually be able to get credit for who you have become. There is power in the parts. God didn't make us in a cast with spiritual plaster. He has literally forged us one piece at a time. Life has mentored you. Circumstances have mentored you. Your process has mentored you. And throughout that process, God has positioned key people to give you seed and wisdom, to give you vision and admonition.

That was the biggest takeaway for me in my formative and developmental years. There has to be more than one person. My best friend, Justin, who I first met when we were fourteen years old, died at the age of twenty-four from non-Hodgkin's lymphoma. I was holding his hand when he took his last breath. His wife and child, my goddaughter, were right there, along with his parents and siblings. I know how David must have felt when his best friend, Jonathan, died. It broke his heart like it broke mine. Like Justin at the time, Jonathan was the only person that truly understood him. He knew his dad, Saul was trying to kill David, and he stayed loyal.

I shared my hopes and dreams with Justin. Growing up there were tons of double dates and other experiences. We went to church and worshipped together. We laughed all the time. I know he would be so proud of what I've accomplished and would have been right here with me if he could. I carry the joy of his life and the pain of the loss with me every day. But there were others that came after him that sowed into me. It's never good to say, "I'm hurt so I'm never going to trust anyone again!" I didn't for a while. I allowed my pain to hamstring me from developing intimate relationships and friendship. I believe that there were people sent by God to help me navigate some of the hard places in my life, but my fear of intimacy caused me to settle for surface relationships. Learn from me, 8s.

So no, I didn't have one man as a mentor. I had multiple men. Many of us didn't have our fathers growing up, so we had to rely on God and other godly individuals to give us wisdom on developing life strategies. Many of those men have children now, some of us are married, others are on their second marriages. But all of us are still loving God and still fighting to serve Him.

I think that David was able to rally men around this common thread: We are all broken but we love God and believe that somehow God's going to turn this thing around. That's the nature of a number 8. Through good or bad, we believe God is going to make a way. And the parts that don't fit now, we don't throw them away. We keep them until later. Because sometimes God will equip you right now for a moment in the future. But you cannot see some stuff. It's not for now. It's literally equipment for later on in the journey. So what we assume is baggage is actually provision. And as we expand, we will see that the parts we've been carrying were necessary so that we can expand our influence, expand the kingdom of God, and ultimately expand into the place called Legacy.

I'm a preacher now and I have a son and a daughter. My

microphone is no longer a scepter. It is not a sign of me arriving. My microphone is a baton, and I'm going to be able to pass it on to my children. So I'm running my race differently now. I have them standing on my shoulders. I didn't have the luxury of standing on the good name of my father, but my children will have my name. It's my prayer that if I live my life right, their dad's name will open doors for them.

Hey, number 8s! Our hearts are our commodities, not our talents. Not our skills. Our brands are our hearts. And it's the parts that seem to be scattered and sewn together in an incongruent pattern that come together in a beautiful mosaic. Just like you, I'm not just one thing. I'm not just a comedian. I'm not just a preacher or a pastor. I'm more than all of that. I'm the man God created. I'm a God creation. That was true for David and that's true for all number 8s. You can't put your finger on one thing that we do. We are called to many things.

Captain of Hearts

David's wilderness experience would have killed most men's spirits. But David wasn't alone. His heart and compassion and leadership were so extraordinary that men followed him into the wilderness. David was the leader of men who were in distress, in debt and discontent. He led men whose hearts had been broken by life. David was the hope of men who had given the best parts of themselves to people who couldn't see them. He was captain of their hearts and the parts of their manhood that were left. And from those hearts and parts grew an army.

Through the crucible of conflict God teaches and trains 8s, moving them from being discontent and in debt, to being disciplined, devoted, and dynamic, in order to give them a life that others can lean on in times of trouble.

Questions for Reflection

1. Was there anyone in your life that was like a David to you? Have you run across any other number 8s who were able to shepherd your broken heart? Share that story if you have it. If not, was there a time where someone tried to serve that role but failed? How did they fail? What did they miss?

2. How do you think a number 8 can help those they are called to serve to actually want to receive help? What are some of the ways we can help those we are called to serve know they are seen and loved?

CHAPTER ELEVEN

My Turn, God's Time

Ministry is not done out of a sense of obligation. It is done from a heart of devotion. There was a time in my life and ministry where I saw myself drifting toward the dead place that many preachers and Christian leaders find themselves in at one time or another: indifference. I saw myself dreading even hearing the phone ring. My phone never stopped ringing, and I felt obligated to answer it every single time. I answered it because when I didn't, people would leave me messages like, "I know you're there, the phone just rang. You just don't want to pick up." This would make me feel guilty and I'd call back all apologetic but wanting to say, "I'm sorry, I was taking a dump and left my phone on the counter. I'll take it with me the next time." Or even better,

"I'm sorry, I was sleeping. I tend to need to do that from time to time. But next time I will stay up and wait for you to call me so I can die an early, sleepless death!" You get the idea. As a minister, everyone wants only five minutes. They don't consider what five minutes multiplied by two hundred people might actually mean.

I'd gotten sick of the rat race. Traveling every other day got tiring, especially when I was single and alone. I can't let girls in the room because God's name and my testimony are on the line. I can't watch the dirty movies, because they cost too much. Wait, just kidding. I mean, they do cost a lot, although I wouldn't know, since I haven't actually ordered one since like 1998. Wait, did I just admit to that? My field life is showing, I suppose. Anyway, there are so many pitfalls awaiting men and women in ministry that I'd gotten to the point that I really thought I was going crazy. I felt like I was going bananas with all of the responsibility that was on my shoulders.

God should put up a disclaimer before calling people into full-time ministry. I think it should read something like this:

> *Help wanted. Pay is great. Eternal benefits. Brokenness is prerequisite. Acknowledgment of My Son is a must. Must be faithful to the end. Hazardous work conditions. Office space is filled with serpents, scorpions, and legions of devils. Also there are fake friends to watch out for as well.*

This job could cost you your life. It will definitely cost you your will. Prayer is a must on and off the job. Fasting is essential. Fighting is encouraged. But the only fight I will ask you to fight, according to my Employee Manual, is the fight of faith.

Must be a skilled wrestler. Spirits and principalities are waiting to be slammed to the ground and defeated. Once you accept your position, it is for life. Must submit to people who get on your nerves and have limited vision. Must work in team settings with idiots from time to time. Can't punch team members in the face or spit on them no matter how much you might want or need to. Must exhibit the fruit of the spirit (see Galations 5:22–23).

For promotion, additional requirements must be met. Must be willing to work longer hours for sometimes less pay. Must be willing to lay down your life for the above-mentioned idiot who has now graduated from idiot to full-blown enemy. Must pray for your enemies and love them unconditionally.

Please, no fat people. No, of course I don't mean in the natural. I mean, no spiritually fat people. Reference Deuteronomy 32:15 in the manual for more information on that. And you cannot apply for promotion. I will elevate you Myself upon completion of your necessary fieldwork. You won't see Me, ever. If you do, it's because you're dead.

Any questions must be directed to Me via My Son.
NO EXCEPTIONS! You are not allowed any off days.
Everyone works every day for as long as your lungs
contract in and out. If these terms are acceptable, I
would love to have you. Sign your life over to Me at your
closest altar. Or right where you are would be fine too.

Thank you in advance for your commitment. You
have chosen the best Company that has ever existed!
Your benefits are immediate and your opportunity for
growth is exponential. I will see you upon completion of
all assignments and pay you for any outstanding balance
owed to you. I look forward to meeting you at the end of
time. We will have forever to catch up.

Sincerely,
The Most High

"Oh sure, sign me up," I think.

I'm fairly certain that the real issue I was having during this frustrating time in my ministry life was that I didn't want to wait my turn. I didn't want to be stuck shaking the hands of five hundred people, giving up a thousand minutes of my time. I wanted God to elevate me above what I believed to be the grunt work of ministry. "I'm not in the field anymore," I thought. "This was fine in the Homeless Shelter," I reasoned. But I'd already been called and anointed. I was supposed to be doing more. But God said I wasn't ready yet—and I wasn't. I had the gift but I didn't quite yet have the character that was needed to keep at the levels God wanted to take me. There was still work to do. Just as David had to wait many years after his anointing in Jesse's house before he could take the throne, I had to wait my turn. And I would soon learn that all the things I was complaining about then, were things that wouldn't be a blip on my radar at the next level.

How to Wait Your Turn

Shepherd David was tending sheep; fighting lions and bears; learning his craft as a musician; sharing his heart with God, all while he was in the field. When he came out of the field he was chased and emotionally exhausted by the man he'd grown to call "father" but who he'd ultimately replace. There were way too many years of fighting for his life.

I'm sure David hated that field at first. It symbolized rejection and isolation. And if you read any of his Psalms of lament, you'll see that David was also not very fond of his time postanointing and prerule either. That time symbolized misunderstanding and disregard. It represented an overwhelming weight of responsibility with no recognition. It was the place that reminded him of his outsider status.

But thankfully, David learned to discern the voice of the Living God. He learned about God's time—*kairos*. The *kairos* moments are the perfect convergence of natural circumstances and spiritual maturity. *Kairos* time is what allows a number 8 to wait their turn. You don't sweat the small stuff, like how many times people call you or how many hands you have to shake. You can relax and give your life and purpose over to God. It doesn't mean you don't set boundaries or that you are sitting around, sleeping in all day, partying all night. It doesn't mean you don't care what happens next or that you aren't seeking opportunities, going to work, preparing for the next thing. You continue doing what you do and trust God for your future. Timothy Keller says in his devotional, *Songs of Jesus*, "Waiting on God, rather than jumping the gun by taking matters into your own hands, is the epitome of wisdom, as the contrasting lives and destinies of Saul (1 Sam. 13:8–14) and David (1 Samuel 26:10–11) make clear."

I know it is hard to wait. But there's comfort in knowing that every battle must end. Every king must be replaced. Every leader gives way to another leader. The plan of succession would be so much easier if power wasn't so corruptible. Men hunger for that which doesn't belong to them. People attempt to hold on to positions of power and the accompanying influence as if their lives depend on it. However, number 8s have been trained to supernaturally wait on God's timing for anything that looks like elevation. Number 8s have learned the hard way that to wait on God is to be maligned and misunderstood by people. But 8s are patient. Quietly, intuitively, they know their moment will come. They don't want the position, the platform, or the spotlight until God gives it.

Questions for Reflection

1. Have you ever not waited patiently on God's timing for your elevation? Be specific. What were the consequences of that? What did you learn from that experience?

2. In what ways can a number 8 learn to "wait their turn"?

CHAPTER TWELVE

Blind Spots

One of the challenges for David wasn't ascension to leadership or being a king. It wasn't that his ascension didn't anesthetize him from his issues. I think what makes David so relatable to me is that God is fully aware and never makes a choice without knowing the outcome. Without knowing the full frame and scope of an individual, God knew that David could be trusted. He also knew that David was broken and would remain that way. I'm always fascinated by the concept of divinity partnering with humanity to bring about God's glory. It is such a weird mathematical equation. God chose to partner with man to bring about a full picture of His glory. David was a precursor and forefather to Jesus. Jesus came from the bloodline and the throne of David. So what was it about David that was so significant?

Regent College's Marketplace Institute's study on David looked at his character specifically:

Character—the inner condition of the human heart is not only something most important to God, it is the most important qualification for political office. So what did God see plainly—and Samuel only dimly at first—when He looked at David's heart? God saw a servant heart, a self-sacrificial heart. David faithfully served his father, his king, and his people. He is frequently referred to in the Scriptures as "God's servant" (e.g., Psalm: 78:70). He was prepared to lay down his life for his flock, his king, his country, and his God—like "the good shepherd who lays down his life for the sheep" (John 10:14–15). Many centuries later the "son of David" would also demonstrate these qualities of heart, declaring, "The Son of Man did not come to be served, but to serve, and to give his life as a ransom for many."

Yes, he was a warrior, a worshipper, and an artist. Overall his character could be trusted. But David had some blind spots. And you'd think that those deficiencies would be things that God wouldn't want to engage. But God did. When David slept with Bathsheba and killed Uriah (see 2 Sam. 11) that didn't catch God off guard. God didn't cover His mouth and gasp. He wasn't surprised. And be clear: the kings of Israel were never supposed to have multiple wives.

God knew that foreign wives would become a snare. However, David had numerous foreign wives, including Bath-sheba. He had his share of women in his lifetime. And if I had to guess, I think you could trace his relational blind spots all the way back to Michal, his first love.

Though he had been anointed, before toppling Goliath, David was an unknown. A kid in the field. Suddenly, he was a war hero and the buzz was going around about him. He had no chance of being in the palace and marrying the daughter of the king before. But one of the perks of beating Goliath and the Philistines was that you were exempt from taxes and you got to marry the king's daughter. But David already had a crush. She was a prize. A beautiful woman. David truly desired her and it was nothing for him to go after her. When David killed Goliath, his fame began to grow.

Check it: Saul didn't give Michal to David right away. Saul had already begun to see David's popularity and wanted him killed. So he told David that if he wanted to marry Michal, he had to bring him a hundred Philistine foreskins. And David brought them to him. Now what! Saul had to give his daughter to David, which in a strange way was a concession that David would take the throne.

One problem though: Michal was who David wanted, but she wasn't good for him.

For me, one of the greatest deficiencies or blind spots, like David, was in the area of relationship. Not being mature and not understanding how to engage, I never asked the right questions, and I hadn't built the necessary adeptness in creating healthy platonic relationships that could possibly lead to something more. Being the guy that never had any kind of attention at key moments in my adolescence, I didn't mature properly. I know now that my early rejection was formative. Some of us don't heal past the point of our first rejection. That's why so many men get caught up rekindling romances with people from their past via Facebook and other social media. They may have thought they were happily married, but because they weren't healed in the place of their first rejection, they go out looking for closure and/or affirmation. It's like the geek who becomes the hunk, or the chubby girl who becomes the beauty queen. It's like going back to the class reunion and everyone saying "Hey, look how you turned out." The only thing is that you really don't want them to love and want the you that you are today, the you that you are in the moment. You want them to retroactively have loved the old you.

I think David not feeling valuable in the early years of his life affected his relational approach. Maybe early on, he wasn't accepted by women. I know what that's like. I know what it's like to desire people who don't desire you. And when you finally do get that attention from someone it's easy to express yourself in inappropriate ways.

As a number 8, I've always been able to "see" people. I could discern the emotions of people. It was a gift. And once I figured out I could home in on the emotional side of a woman's heart, I would use that to get in. Clearly, I wasn't a player or a mack. I really didn't have that skill set. And there's that pesky detail of me not having sex.

My mama made it clear to me at thirteen years old that I would be a virgin on my wedding night. That was fine with me because I didn't really know what sex was then. We didn't have those kind of conversations when I was growing up. So I was like, "Sure!" I wanted to make my mother happy and I didn't want God mad at me. But the unintended consequence of that is sex became taboo. It was like a dirty word. And so this idea of sinful sexuality became a kind of obsession because there was no balance to what I learned about sex growing up. That proved unhealthy because I didn't have a safe place to explore the things I was feeling and thinking without the religious crowd becoming judgmental. So like us 8s tend to do, I internalized it all. I tried to figure things out on my own. And when you are your own counselor, you're in trouble. I was trying to manage emotions that I wasn't equipped to define.

And I think David may have fallen into that same category. He loved Michal, but she still very much had her father's spirit. That was no more evident than when David was bringing the ark of God back into the city. He was so happy that he began to worship. He worshipped so much that he nearly came right out of his clothes. The Bible says that Michal was watching David worship in the streets below the palace and basically became indignant and enraged. David, on the other hand, gave all the city a portion of the spoils. He said, "Go make merry in your homes and rejoice!" But when David came home to bless his house, before he can get the words out, Michal says, "Look how the King of Israel has behaved in front of his maid servants. Behaving as one of the base fellows." She disrespected David because she didn't understand his need to worship. It made no sense to her carnal mind. Michal never understood his heart. That is why she never understood his worship.

I would urge men to be careful about establishing intimate relationships with women who despise your worship. If she despises your worship, she will never be able to help you birth your vision. Conversely, for women, if a man is uncomfortable with your worship of God, you can be certain that there will be places of intimacy that have yet to be fully formed. Search that out before you make a decision to let that person in your life.

So before David could get the blessing out of his mouth, Michal spoke against him. David basically responded with, "It's because God chose me over your father and all his house to bless this place, that's the reason why you say these things." He meant: This has been in you all along! You've secretly hated me all along! You think what I did down there was worship? I'm going to become even more undignified. Even in my own eyes. Because the one thing I won't do is have prideful worship. I will not give God a portion so I can make other people feel comfortable. The Bible goes on to say that Michal was barren after this exchange until the day she died. God wasn't going to allow her to birth his legacy. She mocked his worship and lost the opportunity to carry who he was into the next generation.

From that one rejection, you begin to see David making bad decisions in relationships. The pain of rejection will create a blind spot. It's very important for number 8s to identify those blinds spots so that we don't make a permanent decision based on temporary pain.

The situation with Bathsheba was also a blind spot. A horrible, terrifying blind spot. He was supposed to be at war. "It was at the time when kings go to war." Yet he's on the balcony and he sees Bathsheba bathing. He asks who it is and is told that it is Uriah's wife. Uriah was one of David's mightiest soldiers. One of his top warriors and best security personnel. But what's not stated in the text? How close was Uriah's house such that he could see Bathsheba bathing? In this culture, it would have been extremely frowned upon for a woman to be bathing in broad daylight in a place where she could be easily seen in full view of any man, but especially the king. Was it a setup by Bathsheba? We can't say. Was Uriah's family so close to the king's family that they lived in that kind of close proximity? Who knows? But whether it was the former or the latter, David's experience with rejection blinded him to the possibility of being set up or having compassion for one of his greatest men. Maybe he sent for her because as king he couldn't be rejected, and that would soothe his wound for the moment.

Relational Blindness

Again like David, my relational blind spots are many. I've gotten involved with people who were not beneficial. These weren't relationships that produced a healthy harvest for my life. But something in me was always drawn to them. I was drawn to women who had been fractured in relationships, women who were emotionally drained, maybe even emotionally or mentally abused. These were women who didn't have a lot of financial means. I was drawn to brokenness. Well, they say you attract who you are.

While I'd begun to be a financial success, whatever that means, something in me still identified with these women's brokenness. God was saying to me, "This isn't healthy, John. You are actually projecting yourself onto people who you feel like you need to heal." And that was true. I think I wanted to save them. I think I made myself into a kind of Christ-type, a redeemer. I wanted to be who their last man wasn't. I wanted to be who their children's father wasn't. I had a savior syndrome, knowing full well that there is only one Savior. But this pattern of behavior actually came from me wanting to be saved. I figured a person who was so severely broken wouldn't be able to see my brokenness and would only see me reaching out to them as this wonderful thing. But truth be told, I was just as fractured as they were. I just masked it better.

Number 8s have to guard against our blind spots, whether they are relational, emotional, or spiritual. We have to ask

God what are the things that are missing so that we don't limp through life. So we are able to walk through life whole.

When I first met my wife, I was very judgmental of her. She was volunteering at our church as one of the leaders of the dance ministry. I was leading our youth and our singles ministries. I judged her because she had tattoos. I remember thinking, "Well, if she has tattoos then maybe she just got saved. Maybe she used to be a stripper and God radically changed her life. Maybe that's why she danced with such passion." I'd created a whole narrative about her that had more to do with the state of my mind and heart than anything. It never occurred to me that she got her tattoos when she was sixteen and that she was actually a college graduate working in the health care industry. I wouldn't have known any of that because I had already prejudged her based on a surface glance. I had already deemed her unworthy.

But there was something different about her.

I never knew her name until January 2009, although I'd been around her for about a year. We had a conversation after church that day. She'd just choreographed a dance to a song, and the spirit of God moved so mightily that people were rushing to the altar. When I looked to my left, she was standing there, and I realized that I still didn't know her name. I'd interacted with her but had never asked her name. I don't know what came over me but I grabbed her hand in that service and began to worship.

And since she didn't slap me, I figured it was God.

After church, as she was headed to her car, I asked if I

could speak to her and she obliged. I told her how blessed I was by her dance gift and asked her about her motivation. While she was talking—and I'd never done this before—I asked to borrow her phone, and she gave it to me. I called myself from her phone and left a message saying, "This is wifey's phone!" That's how I got her number.

That night I texted her and asked if we could talk. I waited a couple of hours and she texted me back and said, "I'm going to bed, are you going to call?" So I called her and we talked for the remainder of the night. That meeting in January 2009 would culminate into a proposal in July of 2010. A proposal that in March 2010, God had given me explicit permission to do. See, I needed God to direct me. Before I got to know the woman who would become my wife, I'd been making some really poor relational decisions. I'd come close to putting myself at risk for losing my testimony and credibility. I wasn't sure what love was. I thought physical attraction was love because I hadn't developed beyond my first rejections as a teenager—most of which were because of physicality. I hadn't developed past my first girlfriend in seventh grade breaking up with me after a few days to go with another guy. I hadn't developed past the time in ninth grade when a girl I'd asked to go out with me made me wait a whole twenty-four hours just to tell me no. Those seemingly small rejections affected me deeply. And so when I started becoming known and started receiving a kind of attention I'd never experienced before, that felt good, and I started making unwise decisions. Decisions that didn't honor my real faith. There was an epic battle between my flesh and spirit. I wanted to do right but didn't know how. So the blind spots really got me. Without God intervening, I'm not sure I wouldn't still be in a holding pattern, trying to figure out what real love is. Love isn't just a feeling in the pit of your stomach or the response of your body to another. Love is the sacrifice and the development of true intimacy over time. And sometimes that intimacy doesn't even have a physical response connected to it—at least not initially. God had to free me from my blind spots in order to get me to my destiny.

I want to encourage you by letting you know that God is fully aware of the blind spots in life. And out of His love, He is not going to allow those blind spots to stop you. God knew that David had a relational blind spot, but He didn't let it stop him. David was still able to be used by God. To be called a man after God's own heart. The same goes with you. The mistakes you have made, the things you wish you could go back in time and change, places of remembrances that haunt you, all of those what-ifs, God can still use. You have to leave the land of what-if, though. The land of what-if is a lie. There is no alternate ending.

Don't Disregard Friendships

I lost so many value-adding friendships because I was immature in my emotions, and I filtered every woman I had a feeling for or an attraction to through the lens of romance and my search for "the one." Bishop Donald Clay out of Pittsburgh once said to me, "John, some people are just your friends. Everybody is not the one. In fact, everybody except the one, is not the one. You have to learn how to develop and foster friendships with women that don't have anything to do with attraction."

Truthfully, I thought that was such a weird idea. My thought was that you either find a girl attractive or you don't. And if you find her attractive, you pursue her. It was a very linear way to look at life and relationship. It's also very shallow. But if you don't have a template and no one there to teach you, you navigate the relational landscape the best you can. One of the things I wish I could have done differently, if I could, is to have honored who God sent into my life for who they were in that season and built whatever friendship I was supposed to have had. I missed out on a lot of great exchanges and development of ideas because I was too immature in my emotions.

I also think that my idea of "the one" has changed. I used to be very rigid and conservative in my relational theology. I believed that there was only one person God created for you. That was easy for me because that was the way I classified relationships. But I don't believe that now.

Make no mistake; I am blessed with a fantastic wife and beautiful children. But I was engaged before her and she was engaged before me. And while I believe that there is a purpose in our coming together, she could have just as easily made another decision, and God would have still gotten her to her destiny. See, God has factored in all of our decisions in getting us from "here" to wherever "there" might be. Although we could have made different decisions, the decision we made and the accompanying fruit is exactly what God knew would happen. I do believe that if either of us had made a different decision, we would have still ended up where God wanted us to be, if our hearts were pure.

Now if you have a wicked heart, determined to just not honor God, then that's altogether different. With all the many variances in human emotions, it can be easy to feel like you missed things. There are times when I have felt like I missed something. But I got to believe that God knows how to redeem those moments. Don't look back over your life, wondering what if or wishing that you'd made a different choice. You are where you are supposed to be, and whatever has yet to be reconciled, there is enough time left in your life for God to redeem it. It's only through the vision of God, the clarity of focus through the Holy Spirit, that blind spots become blessings.

Balance Is Everything

Your greatest challenge in being a number 8 is fighting for balance between the call of God on your life, and your family and close relationships that require nurture and attention. Every 8 has a blind spot. If you're able to identify the blind spot (or spots) and address them head-on, you will find life more fulfilling and more joyous.

Questions for Reflection

1. Share one of your blind spots, something that is either connected to your past or your time in the "field." How are you working to overcome these blind spots?

2. How do you find balance between your ministry or work and your family? What specific "checks" do you implement in order to make sure you are not out of order? What are some specific steps that readers can take to do the same?

CHAPTER THIRTEEN

Worshipping Wounded

It was June 22, 2011. I was in Virginia Beach, Virginia, preparing to preach at a church when I got a phone call from my mother at about seven o'clock at night. The call came right before I was about to go out and preach. In fact, I was literally on the side of the platform.

Mom said, "Listen, John. I haven't been feeling well for the past couple months. I didn't want to tell you about it until I talked to a doctor. I have your aunt Sherry on the phone."

I could tell something was wrong by the tone of her voice and my heart felt like it was beating a mile a minute. "What's going on, Mom?" I asked.

She went on to tell me about some tests she'd had the doctor run a couple of weeks prior.

"They are saying there's a growth that has metastasized."

What did she just say to me?

"John, they don't use words like that unless it's cancer but they won't officially tell me anything until tomorrow."

The pastor was literally onstage, introducing me. My heart, beating wildly only a minute before, had nearly stopped.

Mama continued. "I just wanted you to be aware, so you can be praying for me. I didn't want to keep you in the dark any longer."

I hadn't been home to Cincinnati in a while. It's as nice a place as any, I guess. But it's not conducive to dreamers, so I didn't always look forward to going back. I was newly married, and I guess Mom didn't want to add to the stress of a man who was trying to figure out how to live in community with another person after being an only child for thirty-seven years. That's the only reason I could think of as to why she withheld the news from me for so long.

I need you to understand something. Alice Gray was my world. She was my everything. When I was growing up, Mama was the first true Christian I ever knew. She prayed every morning and every night. She studied the word daily and lived out its principles. She served God with her gifts and served others. She was a faithful tither and the church pianist. Yes, I was married and preaching all over the world, but I still needed my mama. I needed her wisdom. I needed to glean from her life. And here was this wicked disease called cancer trying to take her away from me. Cancer lies.

At its worst, it kills. At the very least, it robs you of your joy. Cancer was trying to take my mama and I had to go preach. In the moment of my darkest pain, I had to now lift my hands and lead a crowd of people into the presence of God after hearing the worst news that any child could ever hear.

But my mama, being who she is, said, "And you STILL better go preach the word! God is taking care of me."

And I did. I preached Jesus that night. I lifted my hands, I cried my tears, and I worshipped until there was nothing left. But I'll be honest; I was beyond worried. I still hoped that this was just a nightmare that I was going to soon wake up from.

Nevertheless, I had to worship while I was wounded because that's all I had. I didn't know what the outcome was going to be.

When All Else Fails

As I've mentioned before, there's a duality to being a number 8. David was both a warrior and a worshipper. But it wasn't always easy to be the latter.

When David and his men arrived home at their town of Ziklag, they found that the Amalekites had made a raid into the Negev and Ziklag; they had crushed Ziklag and burned it to the ground. They had carried off the women and children and everyone else but without killing anyone. When David and his men saw the ruins and realized what had happened to their families, they wept until they could weep no more. David's two wives, Ahinoam from Jezreel and Abigail, the widow of Nabal from Carmel, were among those captured. David was now in great danger because all his men were very bitter about losing their sons and daughters, and they began to talk of stoning him. But David found strength in the Lord his God (1 Samuel 30:1–6).

For David and his men, Ziklag represented everything they ever held close. And it was all gone. Nothing and no one were coming back. Ziklag happened and David had to answer for the lost wives and children of the men that were with him. They were so distressed and brokenhearted that they wept to the end of their strength. They were also bitter. They talked about stoning David, killing him. However, the Scripture says that at his very lowest point, David strengthened himself in the Lord his God.

Where do you find the strength to worship when you don't know if your kids are still breathing? Where do you get the fortitude and faith to lift up a praise to God when, in truth, you're not sure if He's walked away from you or not? Actually, if you look at the circumstances it looks like God may have not just forgotten about David, He may have turned against him completely. And yet, in this moment

David worships. How much oil does it take for worship to be your default setting in your lowest moment? Because what you do in your lowest moment is much more telling than what you do in your highest. David didn't accuse God. He never said, "God you're wrong for this!"

You see, worship doesn't count when everything is all good. Worship is most powerful when you can do it through the pain and unspeakable circumstances of your life. David was a wounded worshipper. He was wounded by a father who didn't see him.

He was wounded by the rape of a daughter at the hands of her half-brother. David was wounded when another son, Absalom, killed his rapist half-brother and led a rebellion against his father in an attempt to take the throne of Israel. Oh, to talk with King David in that moment! David, where did you get the strength to worship? Your son is trying to kill you and you go after God? Not to mention that the baby, a son, conceived during the affair with Bathsheba, also died. So he lost three sons and a daughter to tragic circumstances, and yet the Bible says he was still a man after God's own heart.

Where does that kind of worship come from, number 8?

Here's what I know from my own life and David's: That kind of worship comes from both a desperation for the mercy of God and the knowledge of His sovereignty. A sincere belief in His promise that all things will work out for your good (see Rom. 8:28). It comes from an almost frantic grasping for God. It's like you're drowning, and even if you believe God is the one with His hand on your head, you still reach for Him because you know that He is the only one that can save you.

I've noticed this phenomenon with my own son. When I correct him or discipline him sternly, he runs toward me. He knows my character and he knows that this punishment won't last. He knows that I'm going to love him and hold him, even if I'm angry in the moment. And you know what? When I'm disciplining him and he runs toward me, it softens my heart.

Somehow my son knows that even though he doesn't like the pain of correction, his dad will not do anything to truly harm him. Something in him knows that his daddy loves him. I think David felt the same way. Even in his worst moments, he felt as though there was nowhere else to go. Whether it was discipline (as in the case of Bathsheba) or a tragic circumstance, he ran toward God because God was all he had.

David's friends were gone. Jonathan had already been killed in battle by now. Saul had been chasing him, trying to kill him. And David still worshipped. Talk about worshipping wounded! How wounded would David have to be that even when Saul was killed by a foreign mercenary looking for a reward, David says, "Why did you think you could just put your hands on the Lord's anointed?" Scripture says David had the man killed right where he stood.

And David wept for Saul. Keep in mind, Saul was trying

to kill David. Their relationship was a tenuous one at best. No one would have faulted David if he'd killed Saul himself. Kill or be killed, right? But David didn't see it that way. He'd had the opportunity to kill Saul once before. Saul had gone into a cave, and David's men said, "Hey, Saul is in there." I can imagine them thinking, "Yes! Finally! We're going to get him!" But what David did in that moment solidified his position on the throne. God said to him, "Do what seems right to you" (see 1 Sam. 24:4). God wanted to see if all the training he'd put David through had produced a leader He could trust.

David cut off the corner of Saul's robe and let him go but not without revealing himself:

David came out and shouted after him, "My lord the king!" And when Saul looked around, David bowed low before him. Then he shouted to Saul, "Why do you listen to the people who say I am trying to harm you? This very day you can see with your own eyes it isn't true. For the Lord placed you at my mercy back there in the cave. Some of my men told me to kill you, but I spared you. For I said, 'I will never harm the king—he is the Lord's anointed one.' Look, my father, at what I have in my hand. It is a piece of the hem of your robe! I cut it off, but I didn't kill you. This proves that I am not trying to harm you and that I have not sinned against you, even though you have been hunting for me to kill me.

"May the Lord judge between us. Perhaps the Lord will punish you for what you are trying to do to me, but I will never harm you. As that old proverb says, 'From evil people come evil deeds.' So you can be sure I will never harm you. Who is the king of Israel trying to catch anyway? Should he spend his time chasing one who is as worthless as a dead dog or a single flea? May the Lord therefore judge which of us is right and punish the guilty one. He is my advocate, and he will rescue me from your power!" (1 Samuel 24:8–15)

Father? My Lord? Talk about a classic abusive relationship!

There's a backstory here. When the already anointed David came into the house of Saul to play his harp and relieve the king from a distressing spirit, David never really left. His friendship with Jonathan, Saul's son, grew, and he was, in a strange way, part of the family. Even after Saul, in jealousy, tried to drive a spear through David's body, David never left (see 1 Sam. 18). This was every bit a kind of Stockholm syndrome. The kingdom had already been prophetically snatched away from Saul and David still would not go get it himself. It's like he was saying, "If God's going to do this he's going to do all of it. I don't want to touch any of it."

In the meantime, he worshipped.

Someone trying to kill him? He worshipped. Living on the run? He worshipped.

The moment his wounds would scab over, something else would rip it apart. And...he still worshipped.

It was David's wounded worship that kept his heart pliable. It's his wounded worship that kept him writing songs that we still sing today. Being wounded is never easy. In Ziklag, David had to strengthen himself. He was isolated and ostracized by those closest to him, but it didn't matter what they said or did. He still found the internal fortitude to lift a praise. That's a number 8 level of desperation, commitment, and passion. David chose to worship even when he felt all alone.

What we do when we are all alone is a true test of our character. Stacy Utecht spoke powerfully to this over at FCCcanton.com:

Worship is hard when we are hurting. We live in a sinful world, which means we are constantly receiving wounds from people and from circumstances outside our control. We experience deep loss: loss of loved ones, loss of pride, loss of dreams, loss of hope. We carry burdens: our own burdens and the burdens of others. We feel the brokenness of relationships and we sense that things are not as they should be. How are we supposed to love and worship a God who seems distant, unloving, or uncaring? Why does it feel like he only takes from us? Why does it seem like he withholds things from us? Why do we experience pain? The answers to these questions are distant, and we cannot bear to lift his name high. The feelings of freedom, praise, and euphoria in His presence are unimaginable. When we are walking through a time of suffering or pain, worship is the last thing on our list of things to do. But you know what I've learned about our lack of desire to worship in seasons of trial?

It's okay.

God knows you. He sees you. Your pain is not offensive to him or hard to understand. He did not design hurt, but he has been there. In the Garden of Gethsemane before he was crucified, he cried so deeply to his Father and pleaded with Him to not have to go through with it. He was not in a position of euphoric worship. He was hurting. He didn't have peace. He was in pain.

If worship is hard for you right now because you are experiencing something difficult, it's okay. There is grace upon grace upon grace for you. The Psalmist grieved over and over again as he uttered words that were real, raw and full of angst. God knows what your voice sounds like when you are desperate. He sees when you are weak. He is with you when you are broken.

Who We Really Are

When I received the news about my mother's health, I rerouted my travel plans to head to Cincinnati instead of Atlanta, where I was living at the time. After only a few hours of fitful sleep, I went with my mother to her doctor's appointment. The primary care physician, a kind man, told us that my mother had stage 4 cancer that had spread from her pancreas to her spleen to her biliary tubes. Then he dropped the hammer.

"There is nothing we can do."

I cried. My aunt cried. My mom smiled.

We went to her oncologist that same day and he confirmed what her primary care had said. "Ms. Gray, you do have stage four pancreatic cancer. There isn't any surgery for this. I can offer you palliative care and make you comfortable, but you will not recover from this. We don't know exactly but you have maybe three to six months."

I cried at that point. No, scratch that, I lost it. And yes, I know there are those who will say, "You're a preacher. What about your faith?" Please be clear: Tears are not the absence of faith, they are the presence of humanity. When Jesus' dear friend Lazarus died, He wept. But He also said, "Show me where you laid him" (see John 11).

But while I was crying, once again, my mother was smiling.

"Has she lost her mind? Has this news made her crazy?" I thought. I finally asked her, "Mommy, why are you smiling?

Her answered floored me. "I'm so excited. I'm so glad he said that there was no hope because now he can't get credit when God heals me."

Now that was the most stunning gut punch to Satan I'd ever seen. Her smile was a form of worship. It was a level of faith I could only hope to have.

They scheduled a short procedure four days later just so they could identify the specific type of cancer she had. In the meantime, we scheduled a family meeting.

The power of God showed up. My mother said God had made her a promise, and He would not and could not break it.

"When you pray for me, don't pray for my healing. Pray for what he has already done. God is going to get the glory!"

My mother declared life over herself. She raised her hands and rejoiced. She was physically wounded, her body, literally dying, and she was worshipping in the spirit. We can be wounded in our hearts and still worship in the Spirit. We can be wounded in our bodies and still worship in our Spirit. We can be wounded in our souls and still worship in our Spirit. Because the wounds are temporary, but the worship is eternal.

So I took a cue from my mother. I left Cincinnati to preach in another state and I worshipped God the entire flight. I told God how much it hurt but I also told Him that I trusted Him. I surrendered my tears and my fears to Him. My mother's wounds had wounded me, and now it was my turn to worship.

I knew my mother was an amazing woman of God. But those acts of wounded worship revealed her true character.

Oh, by the way, on June 27 my mother went in to have her procedure. And after searching for three hours, the doctors came out confused. They could not find the cancer anywhere in her body! Not. One. Cell. The lesions on her liver were gone. The masses on her vital organs were gone! CT scans that showed cancer four days prior came back clear! A team of doctors studied my mother's charts for months! And they couldn't say it, so I will: It was a miracle! My mother worshipped wounded and God responded. He always responds to wounded worshippers. What was metastatic cancer was now just an easily resolved infection.

It's OK, you can go ahead and shout!

In worship, we find our true selves. We are reminded of the vastness of God, the breadth of His plan, and the small but significant role we play in it. God honors our wounded worship. And as we worship, He heals those places that seem to bleed fresh each time a new hurt hits an old wound. No leader gets off the front lines without scars. That is the journey we agree to when we answer God's call. Every place of pain, every tear, every ache produces a note no one has ever heard, a sound no one can replicate, and a strength no one can take away. Number 8s, like David, like my mother, have learned the secret to sanity in an unstable time. Worship while wounded. The attacks may come, but worship wars on our behalf when our words fail us.

Questions for Reflection

1. Recount a time when you had to worship wounded. Be very specific. What was the outcome? How did God show up?

2. If worship is the secret to a number 8's sanity, then what kind of intentionality must you implement to ensure you are not losing sight of God? What can you do specifically?

CHAPTER FOURTEEN

I Can't Believe I'm Here!

I love standing on a platform and seeing the people of God on fire and praising the Lord. When I walk out onto that stage, I am changed. I am no longer John Gray, husband and father. I am John Gray, number 8, who often has a hard time believing that he has the honor of encouraging God's people. I can't believe I have been chosen—anointed—to bring hope through the word of God to His anointed people. To people just like me—number 8s. Why me? How did I get here?

This is the same question King David asked:

Then King David went in and sat before the LORD; and he said: "Who am I, O Lord GOD? And what is

my house, that You have brought me this far? And
yet this was a small thing in Your sight, O Lord God
(2 Sam. 7:18–19).

David was a king. He had been anointed as a youth in
his father's house, endured many trials, and received many
honors before he got to the palace. And even through all of
that, he still could not believe he deserved to be in the place
where God had placed him. God had called him. God
placed him. But, he could not believe it.

I'm sure you can identify with that. You may have
reached your dream job, your hard-won career, your trophy,
your much coveted prize, but when you stop for a moment,
you wonder, "I can't believe I'm here. How did I get this
far?" You're not alone. In fact, you may be worried that others will discover that you don't deserve to be at the top of
your game. Trust me. I know the feeling.

It's called the Imposter syndrome. In the 1970s, psychologists Suzanne Imes, PhD, and Pauline Rose Clance, PhD,
named these feelings we have. High achievers often feel as
though they will be shown to be frauds, in spite of their
hard work and accomplishments. They aren't actual imposters, but it's hard for them to feel as though they deserve to
be at such a high place. Those with imposter syndrome feel
like each time they step out into the arena—no matter their
chosen career—that someone is going to catch on to their
perceived inadequacies and ask them to leave the room.

I get it.

Sometimes those feelings of being an imposter creep up on me. Especially before a big speaking event or major advancement in my ministry. I recognize that some of those feelings come from my perception of my intellectual abilities. I don't have any advanced degrees. As I've shared here, I left college and did not go back. And spiritually, I know that God always had a plan for my life. Hey, isn't that what this entire book has been about? Yet in my quiet moments I still feel like I'm not worthy of the role I've been given in the kingdom because I never studied the Greek, Aramaic, and Hebrew. (Thank God for the millions of Bible translation apps on the Internet!) But just because I didn't go to seminary doesn't mean I can't study the word of God. I believe it's critical that I study to show myself approved (see 2 Tim. 2:15), but it's only when I'm feeling like an imposter that I believe going to seminary is the only way to do that.

But here's what I know: number 8s are not imposters. Imposter syndrome, while a valid analysis of what happens to some of us psychologically, has nothing to do with us. It's Satan's way of convincing us to forget that as a number 8:

1. God ordained you for a real purpose that unfolds in His appointed time (*kairos*);
2. God has given you the weapons you need to fight thoughts and people that try to defeat your purpose;

God's purpose for you is not just for you, it's also for those others who will help to carry it out.

Sharon Hodde Miller on her blog, SheWorships.com, discusses Imposter syndrome and what it means for the Christian:

Imposter syndrome is not a problem because it makes us feel bad about ourselves or causes low self-esteem. Yes, those are certainly negative consequences, but there is something much bigger at stake.

Imposter syndrome is a distraction from action.

Imposter syndrome can stall and even paralyze you. The fear and inadequacy are like weights around your ankles that prevent you from running full speed. Imposter syndrome will keep you stuck on that boat with Peter, focused solely on your failures.

Likewise, imposter syndrome keeps our eyes fixed on our failure, inadequacy, and smallness. As long as we're preoccupied with our inability, rather than God's ability, we'll live lives of fearful restraint with woefully small goals. We'll never plunge deep into the waters of discipleship.

2 Corinthians 10:5 declares, "We demolish arguments and every pretension that sets itself up against the knowledge of God, and we take captive every thought to make it obedient to Christ."

When Imposter syndrome takes hold of you, you take hold of it. Make it obedient to Christ, who died on the cross to justify your belonging. By the blood of Christ, you are not an imposter, but one who bears the very righteousness of Christ.

So let's say bye-bye to Imposter syndrome once and for all. When it tries to creep back into your mind just repeat the three points above over and over to yourself. Speak life back into and over your purpose.

You Deserve the Kingdom

I had no idea that all the everyday stuff I was doing in the field and postanointing was giving me the time I needed to grow into my purpose. I was working in *kairos*: God's appointed time. And *kairos* looks different for each of us. The time you spent working at Burger King was really about teaching you how to overcome the challenges of serving people in a hurry, people with few resources who want it all— and want it their way. While working at Burger King you were able to go home at the end of the day and write. You wrote about what happened during the day, the people you met, the angry words you held back, and how many people were simply grateful for your "service with a smile." Suddenly (translation: many years later), you accept a high-paying job with many people reporting to you. It's only then that you realize that your season of working at Burger King prepared you for this new challenging career with big pay and even bigger responsibilities. You didn't see it coming, but your purpose unfolded in God's time—not as you had scheduled it.

I work hard because that is the example my mother set for me. I couldn't do less because she expected more—and that's what she gave. I have worked hard since I was a boy. Since there were no sheep where I grew up in Cincinnati, I couldn't serve God as David did by faithfully watching his father's sheep. But I was faithful in the church. I sang in the choir and was active in the youth group. God knew He was developing me for the next step—a giant step— that would come. I didn't know that when I was singing in that small church choir, God was preparing me to tour with Kirk Franklin and The Family. When I went to drama class after school at Winthrow High School, that I would be writing, producing, and starring in my own stage play. Mr. Boyd, a white dude with a beard who was cool and married to a black lady, a brilliant dramatic arts teacher, gave me Shakespeare and drew out my love for the dramatic arts. I thought I was learning drama, but I was also learning how to preach.

Yes, I had to wait for God to move me from the pain I felt when I left college, returned in defeat to my mom's house and the church I had left a year before in triumph. But God's promises can be trusted. "God is not a man, that he should lie; neither the son of man, that he should repent: hath he said, and shall he not do it? or hath he spoken, and shall he not make it good?" (Num. 23:19).

Guard Your Thinking

Pastor Aaron Cordeiro says on Enewhope.org,

> What goes on in your head will bear fruit in your world. Can you tell the fruit of your life by your thoughts? What we think in our head comes out of our mouth and our actions. For instance when a person views pornography, he will have a distorted view of the opposite sex and will treat them as objects rather than as a person. It is very important to keep our thought life in check because the health of a person's thought life is critical to leadership.

So number 8s, release those thoughts that say, "I'm an imposter." "I don't deserve to have good things." "There are other people who are taller, shorter, can sing better, is a better parent, can preach/teach/minister better than I." Believe that you belong where you are! It will be a battle on some days. And there will be those who will feed those fears of yours. But remember where you should cast cares and get back to the business of doing what God has called you to do.

Here are a couple of Scriptures that have helped me through the toughest battles with Imposter syndrome and will assist you in guarding your own thinking:

For we do not wrestle against flesh and blood, but against principalities, against powers, against the rulers of the darkness of this age, against spiritual hosts of wickedness in the heavenly places (Ephesians 6:12).

Stand therefore, having girded your waist with truth, having put on the breastplate of righteousness, and having shod your feet with the preparation of the gospel of peace; above all, taking the shield of faith with which you will be able to quench all the fiery darts of the wicked one. And take the helmet of salvation, and the sword of the Spirit, which is the word of God; praying always with all prayer and supplication in the Spirit (Ephesians 6:14–17).

These verses in Ephesians are extremely critical when guarding your thoughts against the lies of the devil. Truth is the first protection you put on to prepare for battle. You begin by speaking the truth. Number 8s speak the truth with love, which allows us to be a witness for the Lord with freedom because our actions are being watched. Next, is the "breastplate of righteousness." A breastplate protects all your important organs. Righteousness keeps you focused on Jesus who died and rose so you could live in right relationship with God. We must rely on Jesus to keep that armor from being busted open by sin.

When your feet are covered in peace, you have contentment in your relationship with Jesus. You know how peaceful a baby looks when she is sleeping on her mother's lap?

Well, that is the kind of peace available to us when we rest in the knowledge that Jesus loves us and is keeping us protected from spiritual warfare. But you must remain close and rest in His care.

Your shield and helmet both offer protection from fiery darts of doubt, mistrust, and any thoughts that keep you from feeling secure in God's love and salvation. This is especially good when the enemy tries to attack your mind with thoughts of you not being good enough. Have the same trust in God that Shadrach, Meshach, and Abednego had when placed in the fiery furnace for refusing to worship other gods. Shadrach, Meshach, and Abednego said, "If that is the case, our God whom we serve is able to deliver us from the burning fiery furnace, and He will deliver us from your hand, O king" (Dan. 3:17). Say aloud or in your heart, "If what you say is true, Satan, then God can make me enough. Case Closed."

Your most important and strongest weapon is the Word of God. Read your Bible daily. Gain strength from the prophets, who kept preaching regardless of what happened to them. Regardless as to whether they felt they were capable or not. You will probably not be shipwrecked like Paul (see 2 Cor. 11:25), thrown down a muddy well like Jeremiah (see Jer. 38:6), or swallowed by a whale like Jonah (see Jon. 1:17), but you will have people trying to get you off course. You will have those whispers of inadequacy in your mind. By staying in the Word you will be able to resist and stand against all of these falsehoods.

Finally, pray. Pray without ceasing. Pray and know that God hears your prayers and is faithful to answer them. *Kairos* time or Chronos (clock) time—you can trust God for an answer. Jesus said, "If you ask anything in My name, I will do it" (John 14:14).

As I've noted here, one of the most challenging battles you will ever fight is the battle for your thoughts. The Good News translation gives this reading to Proverbs 4:23: "Be careful how you think; your life is shaped by your thoughts." Change your thinking about being an imposter; don't let thoughts enter your mind that work to convince you that you are less than God made you to be. Just as David fought repeatedly against his enemies, you must constantly fight against listening to words from anyone, including yourself, that cause you to doubt God's anointing of you or the purpose that He plans to complete in you (see Phil. 1:6). Be confident of your purpose. Go to battle whenever your thoughts begin to overcome your faith. You have had many victories because of God's favor, because God has a purpose for your life.

When you've come a long way like I have, it's impossible to stand up front and not be amazed at what God has done in your life. Let's be very clear: I know I'm not an imposter because God had already laid the groundwork for my success. You are not an imposter because God already gave you a purpose and anointed you for success. I know this because even while David was still tending sheep and sleeping in fields, God had already ordained that he was to be crowned king of Israel.

God's Love: From David to Jesus

God is sovereign, for sure. And it's easy to get so caught up in feeling like an imposter in light of His power and might that you forget that His love for us goes deeper than the deepest sea. Remember even King David wondered if a God as powerful and wise as Jehovah would even notice him. Why would God notice such a flawed man? But God also has another trait: God is love. God's love is from everlasting to everlasting (Ps. 103:17) and will never fail. When you remember the love of God for you, then you can remember your biggest strength—your biggest weapon—to fight thoughts that keep you from enjoying your success. You are God's beloved.

As King David inquired of the Lord in the verse above, he might have thought back over his younger days and about the many victories he had won in the name of the Lord. David won many victories over the Philistines, the Amalekites and their allies in Syria, the Moabites, Edom, and Zobah to name a few. Sometimes it's important to remind ourselves how God has shown up for us when we are struggling with hearing Him.

Out of all the things to be grateful for, David had his

lineage. I imagine God saying, Who are you, David? You are the spiritual lineage through which I will bring my Son, Jesus, into the world. There was no way for him to know it at the time, but David was a precursor of the Messiah. He was born in Bethlehem. His family wasn't special. No one saw Him coming. He was anointed by God and both hated and celebrated by men. By the time it was all said and done, the nation and the world were never the same! A King had taken the throne! Do I speak of David or Jesus? The stories are so remarkably similar that one could be interchanged with the other.

Your Future as a Number 8

This is the ultimate power of a number 8. The glory that is produced in us is hidden until the exact moment it's needed. Only history will tell the tale of our influence on art, entertainment, education, culture, science, academia, and technology. Being a number 8 is not just an ethereal, spiritual enigma; it's a truth wrapped in flesh. God will take the hidden and make it become the thing men seek out worldwide. God will hide His anointing in plain sight and cause us to seek Him for wisdom, answers, and direction. The full potential of a number 8 will never be actualized without God. He will hide gifts inside us that only pain and process can unearth. God the Father hid His Son in Bethlehem, not unlike the way He hid His choice for King of a nation many years before that. David, Jesus, and you. Implausible, impossible, and improbable, but nonetheless quite real. We are number 8s. Hidden no longer.

Questions for Reflection

1. Have you experienced Imposter syndrome? In what areas? How has it affected the way that you pursue your goals and purpose?
2. Going forward, how will you prepare for the transition from "being hidden" to God revealing you as his anointed?

Acknowledgments

I remember asking my mother to help me buy a laptop back in the year 2000 for the sole purpose of writing my first book. I told her my premise and she laughed with so much joy and delight in the possibilities. She gladly spent over two thousand dollars on that laptop because she was convinced of my dream. Mommy told me that when my book came out, the world would be blessed. It was hard to internalize her lofty words, yet her confidence reassured me that God wanted me to write what was in my heart. Seventeen years later, that laptop may be out of date, but not what my mom invested in—finally being shared with the rest of you.

Why did it take so long, you might ask? I've learned that the best books are lived before they are written. True transformation takes place when information collides with revelation. Until I had lived the chapters, they couldn't come together correctly. After much time and many tears, I know in my heart that now is the time.

I am indebted to so many people who helped me along this journey. I want to thank Dr. Wayne R. Davis, the pastor of Bethel Baptist Church in Ohio, under whose leadership I gave my life to Christ and haven't looked back. His mix of relatable teaching mixed with credentialed knowledge and biblical foundation was my first introduction to the power of the preached word. I want to thank Dr. Michael Dantley, pastor of Christ Emmanuel Christian Fellowship in Ohio, for introducing me to "The More" of God in the person of the Holy Spirit. My life and ministry trajectory were never the same once I began to understand the power available to me. I want to thank Bishop Donald Clay of Petra International Ministries in Pennsylvania for covering me and sowing into me at the most vulnerable time in my young ministry life. I had made some life-altering decisions that, to many, seemed crazy at the time. But you assured me that I had heard from God. Without your revelatory insight and financial support, I don't know how that season in my life would have turned out.

I want to thank Dr. DeForest Soaries, Jr. of First Baptist Church of Lincoln Gardens in New Jersey for giving me my first full-time position as a youth minister. It was during my time with you that God first spoke to me about writing a book. Thank you for taking a chance on a very green minister who had so much to learn. To Bishop Donald Hilliard, Jr. of the Cathedral Second Baptist Church in New Jersey, thank you for giving me a place to call home as God was preparing me for the next phase of my life. Your mix of passion, pastoral love, and commitment to biblical orthodoxy (Maundy Thursday) and liturgy showed me that I could be passionate without sacrificing scriptural foundation. I also want to thank Bishop Vaughn McLaughlin in Florida for seeing in me a greatness that was beyond my limited vision at the time—and then seeding that greatness with growth opportunities and necessary structure. To Dr. James L. Morman of Christian Tabernacle Church in Michigan, you have been a father to me and prophetically spoken over me things that only God Himself could have shown you, and they've all come to pass. I honor you and I'm forever grateful for your wisdom, insight, and keen prophetic eye. I hope I make you proud.

To pastor Hart Ramsey, Sr. of Northview Christian Church in Alabama, thank you for ordaining me an elder in the Lord's Church and legitimizing what God had been doing all along. No one teaches the Word like you. To Bishop Eugene Reeves of The Life Church in Virginia, I love you for your fatherly wisdom, prophetic prayers, and declarations that are still coming to pass, and for your love for your wife and children and grandchildren. You are a rare and wonderful man of integrity, and I'm honored to be called a son.

To Bishop Carlton Brown of Bethel Gospel Assembly in New York, God only knows what you mean to me. Thank you for always being there. To Dr. A. R. Bernard, Sr. of Christian Cultural Center in New York, I am overwhelmed by the level of authority, balance, knowledge, wisdom, and depth you have. How you can be so many things at the same time is patently unfair, but I'm grateful to know you and call you a critical voice in my life! To Pastor Jentezen Franklin of Free Chapel Church in Georgia, thank you for being an uncompromising voice in a compromising time. My time under your leadership was filled with great moments of growth and revelation in God. To Bishop Eddie Long of New Birth Missionary Baptist Church in Georgia, thank you for giving me the opportunity to serve the youth and singles of your church. It was there that I reconnected with my first passion, which is to see young people running after Jesus Christ with their whole hearts. And it was there that I found my enduring passion—my beautiful wife, Aventer Gray. God bless you and your family always.

And finally to Pastors Joel and Victoria Osteen and the entire Lakewood Church family in Texas, I am honored to be a part of the work of God that began with your mother and father that now continues with the both of you. Your faith in me, and the consistent example of love, kindness, humility, and grace while living out your calling has inspired me. The level of discipline and commitment it takes to do what you do globally will not be seen by most, but I've observed it well and I stand and call you blessed. Your integrity and love for your family are the most glowing examples of a life well lived. God bless you, pastor, and thank you for allowing me to serve the vision.

This is by no means a full list of people who have been critical to me, but all of these individuals have something in common. They were all at one point or another shepherds in my life. These voices, along with others, helped to shape me into the man I am today. Each one of these voices speaks to different areas of my life. I gleaned what I could from each of them. I hope I honor their investment with the life I live and the way I love my wife and children.

To the amazing Jan Miller and Shannon Marven of Dupree Miller Associates, I can't thank you and the entire team enough for helping me navigate the publishing landscape. Your love for what you do and the way you went above and beyond to help me get this first book out will never be forgotten. To my editor Adrienne Ingrum, I love you. Your patience with me is the stuff of legend. You are the best at what you do and I could not have had a better voice pushing me to complete this monumental task. Your brilliance is all over this book. Thank you. To Tracey Michae'l Lewis-Giggetts, there are simply no words for what you were able to help me accomplish. Your genius, insight, gift with words, and late night e-mail exchanges helped me to fulfill a lifelong goal. God bless your wonderful husband and beautiful daughter for the time they sacrificed to allow you to come alongside me to help your brother to the finish line.

To Rolf Zettersten and the entire FaithWords/Hachette publishing family, especially production editor Melanie Gold, thank you for believing in me. I believe this is just the beginning of great relationship that will produce much fruit and bless many souls. Honored to call this place my publishing home. Finally, I want to thank my entire family and all my friends for every prayer they've ever prayed and word of encouragement they've given. Each word pushed me and catapulted me to where I am today. I stand on the prayers of my grandmothers, Mayme Davis and Celestine Gray. I stand on the prayers of Alice Gray, a mother who never gave up. And I stand on the prayers of a wife who believes in me and has laid down her personal vision in order to build the one God gave to me for us. Thank you, Aventer Gray. I love you and the two babies you blessed me with. Daddy loves you, John IV and Theory Aspyn-Sky. I hope you are blessed by this book. It took seventeen years and eight different computers to write!